LEST WE FORGET

MEDITATIONS AT THE MEAL OF REMEMBRANCE

CLINTON J. HOLLOWAY

COLD TREE PRESS
NASHVILLE, TENNESSEE

*The author grants permission that individual meditations from the book
may be may be read aloud for celebrations of the Lord's Supper.*

*Cover image provided by the author.
Lord's Supper detail in Window of the Resurrection,
in the former First Christian Church, Nashville, Tennessee.*

*Proceeds from the sale of this book go to benefit the World Convention
of Churches of Christ (www.worldconvention.org) and Disciples of Christ
Historical Society's Great Communion Celebration (www.greatcommunion.org),
commemorating the 200th Anniversary of Thomas Campbell's Declaration and Address.*

*For information contact:
Clinton J. Holloway
milligan95@yahoo.com*

*Published by Cold Tree Press
Nashville, Tennessee
www.coldtreepress.com*

Library of Congress Control Number: 2008931610

*© 2008 Clinton J. Holloway. All rights reserved.
Cover and Interior Designed by Amanda Butler © 2008 Cold Tree Press*

*Printed in the United States of America
ISBN-13: 978-1-58385-278-1
ISBN-10: 1-58385-278-6*

For Grandma
Who, by example, led me to the cross.

Doris L. Campbell
1912-2003

CONTENTS

ACKNOWLEDGMENTS

In putting together this collection of meditations, I want to recognize the two congregations for whom these thoughts were originally written: Gap Creek Christian Church of Elizabethton, Tennessee and the former First Christian Church of Nashville, Tennessee, now Aspen Grove Christian Church of Franklin, Tennessee. Thank you for the opportunity to serve. Many thanks to Jennifer Taylor, contributing editor for *Christian Standard,* who was my helpful editor. She made countless suggestions and corrections that have made this a much more useable tool. Jeff Weston, Executive Director of World Convention, also read an edition of the manuscript and made many helpful suggestions. Amanda Butler, Senior Designer at Cold Tree Press, has done a beautiful job transforming a dream into book form. To my wife, Adele, for her support, encouragement and love, I am very much indebted. And last, but not least, honor is due to our Lord for his blessing and provision. *Ad Deo Majores Gloria.*

INTRODUCTION

As an undergraduate at Milligan College, I took advantage of the Semester Abroad opportunity, choosing to study at Springdale College in Birmingham, England in the spring of 1994. Each week my friends and I attended several different local congregations, many within our own tradition. (The British Churches of Christ share the heritage of America's Restoration or Stone-Campbell Movement churches.)

Though I had grown up in the church—some parts of my family have been in the Movement for seven generations—the British Churches of Christ exposed me to the idea, and firmly planted my belief, that the Lord's Supper was and is the *central* act of worship. Everything in this book flows from this premise.

THE MEAL'S PRECEDENCE

At Springdale I studied British Church of Christ history and William Robinson, its major twentieth-century figure. Robinson's steadfast assertion of the centrality of the Lord's Supper put him squarely in the Stone-Campbell tradition. In his manual

A Companion to the Communion Service,[1] "W.R.," (as he was called) reminds his readers communion "...is the supreme form of Christian worship offered to God by the Church..." For him, the Lord's Supper took precedence over preaching, singing, music or anything else done by the body for worship.

"To celebrate the Lord's Supper is the most exalted service we ever perform in the Church of the living God," Robinson goes on to say. Likewise, Thomas Campbell, considered a spiritual fore-father of the Stone-Campbell Movement, calls the Lord's Supper "that great sacrament of unity and love" in his *Declaration and Address,* and Alexander Campbell reminds us "He never bade his house to assemble but to eat and drink with him."[2]

The purpose of this book, then, is to provide meditations focusing on the centrality of the Lord's Supper in worship. I take my cues from my beloved seminary professor, Robert O. Fife, himself a student of Robinson, who challenged congregations to "Restore to the Ordinances their proper place in the Community of Faith. Together with the Word, they are the chosen means of God's encounter with His People. Moreover, they exhibit the Gospel in work and deed for all to see."[3]

---

1 William Robinson, *A Companion to the Communion Service.* The Berean Press, Birmingham, England, 1942.
2 Quoted in Robinson, page 53, with no citation. There are some who will argue the first churches coming out of the Reformed (Church of Scotland, Presbyterian) Protestant tradition to restore weekly observance of the Lord's Supper were those of the Restoration or Stone-Campbell Movement. See Tom Lawson, *Communion: Weekly or Weakly?* In *Christian Standard,* June 10, 2007, 7.
3 Robert O. Fife, *Celebration of Heritage,* in *One Body,* Winter 2004, 7.

THE MEAL'S PREPARATION

Robinson believed this important meal should be conducted properly. His manual reminds readers that a high view of the Lord's Supper necessitates adequate preparation for those who serve, in particular, and for all those who commune. Although this decades-old *Companion* can sound harshly didactic today, perhaps our early 21st-century churches could benefit from its substance if not its tone. At the very least, the person called to lead a congregation in preparing for communion with the Lord could benefit from a few reminders. Following the lead of W.R., we offer these:

- The elements should be neither offered nor consumed without personal preparation. Paul cautioned the Corinthian church that whoever eats the bread and drinks the cup in an unworthy manner is guilty of sinning against the body and the blood of the Lord (1 Corinthians 11:27). Therefore, the man or woman who presides at the table with the responsibility to lead the congregation's thoughts has a most important task. For if those who serve are inadequately prepared, or they make the communion a meaningless ritual, they diminish the spiritual benefits of the Lord's Supper for the whole church. Preparation leads to an atmosphere of spiritual benefit.

- The meditation should also be carefully prepared. Whether a speaker composes their own meditation, or adapts a pre-written meditation such as one from this book, they should practice it ahead of time, familiarize themselves with the scriptural passages, and customize the meditation to their congregation. Thus the speaker is better prepared to help the congregation focus its thoughts on Jesus. (And it may seem obvious, but always remember to include Jesus in the communion meditation. I know some speakers who don't!)

- When considering the meditation, the words of institution—that is, the words spoken by Christ when he instituted the meal—are never inappropriate. (The words of institution can be found in the following passages: Matthew 26:26-29; Mark 14:22-25; Luke 22:17-20 and 24:30; and 1 Corinthians 11:23-26. The sixth chapter of John, beginning with verse 35, also provides excellent reference to Christ's words as he prepared the disciples for the first observance of the Lord's Supper.)

- Neither is physically breaking the bread and pouring the cup out of place. Although some congregations have given up these ancient practices, the words of institution and the breaking of the bread can create a very powerful visual effect. Many meditations in this volume include the words if institution. Those that do not can easily be adapted to include them and the physical breaking and pouring of the elements.

- While music is important in the overall worship experience, we should remember that singing during the meditation time, as well as throughout the service, is not done for musical effect or entertainment. Therefore it is not a showcase of talent but an offering of thanksgiving and praise. The music or liturgy, according to Robinson, should be planned with the themes of the day in mind. This may be very difficult in churches without intentional integration of scripture, songs, sermon, and "supper." However, if done well music can be a wonderful tool in directing congregational thought to the Communion. Three appropriate songs, among many, are: Bryan Jeffery Leech's *Come Share the Lord;* Andra Moran's *Come to the Table Again;* and Thom Schuyler's *One Piece of Bread.* Michael W. Smith's *Ancient Words* is another with a theme that lends itself to Communion time.

- While the elements may only be "juice" and "bread" they are physical representations of the broken body and the blood poured out, and those who serve the elements should handle them with respect. Servers should be trained in passing the elements so that when something out of the ordinary happens they are ready to respond with confidence.

- Not found in Robinson's manual, but offered for inclusion here is a word about children. Our tradition has often neglected children in observance of the Lord's Supper. Typically, communion has been reserved for those who have confessed their faith in Christ and been baptized. Until children have reached this understanding they are generally bypassed. However, this moment of congregational worship can also be an instructive time for its youngest members. A valuable resource in educating children about the Lord's Supper is the essay *General Instructions for a Celebration of the Lord's Supper for Children* by Dr. Myron J. Taylor.[4] Another resource is a wonderful children's book (which itself makes an excellent communion meditation) *Hey, God, What is Communion?* By Roxie Cawood Gibson.[5] These two resources will go a long way toward instilling in future generations the centrality of the Lord's Supper in worship and life of the Church.

Dr. Robert O. Fife said it best when he wrote, "Amidst a troubled world, how beautiful is this weekly celebration of remembrance and hope!"[6] I wish you God's blessings as you prepare to lead the hearts of your congregation in the Meal of Remembrance. May you find this, in a troubled world, to be a time of true celebration and the hope of eternal things to come.

Clinton J. Holloway

Nashville, Tennessee

---

4 Dr. Taylor's essay, along with hundreds of his communion meditations, can be found at www.myronjtaylor.com
5 Mrs. Gibson's *Hey, God…*series of children's books are available at www.premiumpress america.com
6 Robert O. Fife, *Why Have Communion Every Week?*, Restoration Alive Series IV, Emmanuel School of Religion leaflet, no date.

LEST WE FORGET

MEDITATIONS FOR
SPECIAL OCCASIONS

YOM KIPPUR: DAY OF ATONEMENT
HEBREWS 10:4-7

"By consent of the authorities in heaven and on earth we permit sinners to enter and be a part of the congregation."

Thus a Cantor begins the service for the Jewish holy day of Yom Kippur. Yom Kippur is not a feast day like most Jewish festival days. Rather it is a day of fasting, repentance, and forgiveness. Yom Kippur is also known as the Day of Atonement, for it is the day every Jew will seek atonement for all the sins of the past year and thus, the next day, begin anew with a slate wiped clean in the eyes of God.

In ancient times, the fasting and prayer were accompanied by sacrifices and burnt offerings at the Temple in Jerusalem. It was the only time of the year the high priest was permitted to enter the Holy of Holies. There, standing before the very presence of God, the high priest would present the sacrifice and ask for atonement for all of the Jewish nation.

The writer of Hebrews reminds us, as Christians whose roots are in Judaism, that no bull or goat is sufficient to atone for our sins. *...because it is impossible for the blood of bulls and goats to take away sins.*

Therefore, when Christ came into the world, he said:

"Sacrifice and offering you did not desire, but a body you pre-pared for me; with burnt offering and sin offering you were not pleased. Then I said, 'Here am I—it is written about me in the scroll—I have come to do your will, O God'" (Hebrews 10:4-7).

This week we have celebrated the coming of the new year. Many see it as a clean slate and the chance to begin anew. Perhaps you have even made a resolution to change some aspect of your life, to be a better person, to be less sinful in the coming year. Chances are you will fail, you will fall short and you will even sin again. But fear not, for we have a hope found in Jesus Christ. God no longer requires us to atone for our sins through the blood of bulls and goats. Jesus paid the price when he went to the cross on Golgotha. He provides a lasting and permanent atonement and sealed it with his body and blood. That is how we have the consent of heaven to gather as sinners and be a part of this congregation, part of the body of Christ.

Then he took the cup, gave thanks and offered it to them, saying, "Drink from it all of you, this is my blood of the covenant, which is poured out for many for the forgiveness of sins." (Matthew 26:27-28).

Let us pray, giving thanks for the atonement of our sins...

FINDING FAITH IN A FLOWER
ISAIAH 35:1-2

There is a philosophy that says God revealed Himself to us in two ways: through His inspired word, the Bible and through His inspired creation, Nature. His beautiful creation of flowers and trees, rocks and streams is said to speak as well of our Lord as any passage of scripture. I think the author of the poem *Finding Faith in a Flower* believed that when she penned these words:[7]

Finding Faith in a Flower
Sometimes when faith is running low,
and I cannot fathom why things are so,
I walk alone among the flowers I grow
and learn the answers to all I would know.
For among my flowers I have come to see
Life's miracles and its mystery
and standing in silence and reverie
My faith comes flooding back to me.

7 Poem by Helen Steiner Rice.

The prophet Isaiah expresses the same sentiments when he writes in the thirty-fifth chapter:

> *The desert and the parched land will be glad;*
> *the wilderness will rejoice and blossom.*
> *Like the crocus, it will burst into bloom;*
> *it will rejoice greatly and shout for joy.*
> *The glory of Lebanon will be given it,*
> *the glory of Carmel and Sharon;*
> *they will see the glory of the Lord*
> *the splendor of our God (Isaiah 35:1-2).*

Soon spring will be upon us and we will see the crocus burst into bloom. Let me invite you to walk among the flowers and there find your faith once more. See in nature the glory of the Lord and the splendor of our God. Remember that the same God who cares for the lily and gives it a splendor greater than that of Solomon does not forget you. The same hands that brought gladness to the desert and parched land are the hands that were nailed to the cross. Jesus invites us to the table of faith.

Let us pray, giving thanks for faith that comes in many forms...

THE LAST WEEK
SELECTIONS FROM MATTHEW

Today is Palm Sunday, the day we observe Christ's triumphal entry into the city of Jerusalem. Palm Sunday also marks the beginning of the most important week in the Christian calendar, the week leading up to Resurrection Sunday. We know more about this week than any other period of time in Jesus' life.

Sunday, Jesus rides the donkey into Jerusalem while the people shout hosannas.

Monday, Jesus curses the fig tree and cleanses the Temple.

Tuesday, Jesus teaches in the Temple and his authority is questioned by the chief priests and the elders. In the evening he is anointed.

Wednesday, the plot against Jesus was formed.

Thursday, Jesus and the disciples partake of the Lord's Supper, Jesus comforts the disciples, and they pray in the Garden of Gethsemane.

Late into the night on Thursday and early in the morning on Friday, Jesus is arrested and a farce of a trial is held before the chief priests, then Pontius Pilate, then Herod, and again before Pilate who orders Jesus' crucifixion to take place that very day.

Friday, Jesus is crucified and dies. His broken body is laid in the tomb of Joseph of Arimathea.

Saturday is the Sabbath. All is quiet while the followers of Jesus mourn.

Sunday, the women go to the tomb and find the body of the Lord is gone. Jesus appears to them in the garden, then to the two on the road to Emmaus and finally to the ten disciples in the locked room.

As we now pause to partake of the meal Christ instituted for the Church on that Thursday night, while they were gathered in the Upper Room, let us remember what this week means as we look forward to Resurrection Sunday. That for our sins Christ left the presence of the Father and for a time dwelt among his creation on Earth, walking among his children until the day when he gave up his brief earthly life so that we might gain eternal heavenly life.

The Lord Jesus, on the night that he was betrayed, took bread, and when he had given thanks, he broke it and said, "This is my body, which is for you; do this in remembrance of me." The same way, after supper he took the cup, saying, "This cup is the new covenant in my blood; do this, whenever you drink it, in remembrance of me." For whenever you eat this bread and drink this cup, you proclaim the Lord's death until he comes (I Corinthians 11:23b-26).

Let us pray, giving him triumphal entry into our hearts...

OH, WHAT A VICTORY!
1 CORINTHIANS 15:50-57

In Jan Karon's best-selling novel *These High, Green Hills,* Episcopalian Rector Father Timothy Kavanaugh muses over the passing of his elderly parishioner Sadie Baxter. He ponders to himself:

> How often had people heard that, for a Christian, death is but the ultimate triumph, a thing to celebrate? The hope was that it ceased being a fact merely believed with the head, and become a fact to be known with the heart...[8]

As we are entering the Holy Week of Christ's Passion we are perhaps more keenly aware of his death than any other time of the year. Do we see death as a finality? The terminus of living? The boundary of life which brings to a close all our mortal journeying? If we do, and at the same time we wear the name of Christian, we fail to understand the meaning of this week.

If we fail to understand that death is the ultimate triumph, we become like Mary Magdalene and the others who lived despondently in those hours between the crucifixion and the resurrection.

---

8 Jan Karon, *These High, Green Hills,* Penguin Books, New York, New York, 1996, 281.

"Why?" rolls over and over in our heads and we wonder with incredulous disbelief at the futility of it all.

Paul wrote in his first Corinthian epistle: *I declare to you, brothers, that flesh and blood cannot inherit the kingdom of God, nor does the perishable inherit the imperishable. Listen, I tell you a mystery: We will not sleep, but we will all be changed—in a flash, in the twinkling of an eye, at the last trumpet. For the trumpet will sound, the dead will be raised imperishable, and we will be changed. For the perishable must clothe itself with the imperishable, and the mortal with immortality. When the perishable has been clothed with the imperishable, and the mortal with immortality, then the saying that is written will come true: "Death has been swallowed up in victory."*

"Where, O death, is your victory?
Where, O death is your sting?"

The sting of death is sin, and the power of sin is the law. **But thanks be to our God! He gives us victory through the Lord Jesus Christ** *(1 Corinthians 15:50-57).*

Let us pray, giving thanks for the victory...

DANDELIONS
JOHN 10:28; 11:25

They come each spring. Nothing is able to stop them indefinitely. No matter where you go, each and every spring, there they are. What am I talking about? **DANDELIONS.** A lowly weed; it is mighty in its persistence and resilience. They have been called the flower of love owing to the fact that it makes up the first bouquet every mother receives from her child.

It is the plant that we pull up, dig out, poison and use all manner and method to destroy. Yet it pops up its bright yellow head time and time again. Lest you think they are wholly without redeeming quality, they do offer some compensation: their roots contain a drug used in treating the liver. The leaves, very rich in vitamins and antioxidants, are prized for spring salads and wine can be made from the flowers.

Rev. Joel Reif says, "I personally think the flower should be the Easter flower. It symbolizes life; the life that God gives us in Christ. Life that is never able to be destroyed."[9]

Jesus gives us his word that life in him cannot be destroyed

---

9 Rev. Joel Reif was Senior Minister of the First United Church of Christ, Bluffton, Indiana, 1992-1997.

when he says, *"I give them eternal life, and they shall never perish; no one can snatch them out of my hand" (John 10:28.)*

We celebrate Easter as a reminder of that promise that life in Christ cannot be destroyed. Jesus himself gave us the proof when he defeated death and walked away from the tomb. Jesus also said, *"I am the resurrection and the life. He who believes in me will live, even though he dies; and who ever lives and believes in me will never die. Do you believe this?" (John 11:25.)* Each week we partake of the Lord's Supper as further reminder of those promises and to affirm our belief, that the life God gives us in Christ can never be destroyed.

Let us pray, giving thanks for life that cannot be destroyed...

IN GOD WE TRUST
JOHN 14:1-3

In eighteenth century America, we the people learned to put our faith in a particular form of government. We the people had twice defeated the British, conquered the vast wilderness territories, and carved out of that raw material the makings of a great nation. We the people had come to put much faith and trust in the federal republic we had created.

But by the 1860s our nation was being torn apart over the issue of slavery. State was pitted against state, the North verses the South, brother against brother. As the country was being torn asunder some came to realize the trust invested in the republic was misplaced.

In 1861, a Maryland resident wrote to Solomon P. Chase, the Secretary of the Treasury, suggesting a new national motto. Chase liked the idea and brought it before Congress. The motto first appeared in 1864 on the two cent bronze coin. In 1865 an act of Congress ordered the Director of the Mint to stamp the motto on all gold and silver coins. Since then **"In God We Trust"** has appeared on all the United States' legal tender.

But the idea did not originate with the Maryland resident. In the fourteenth chapter of John's Gospel, Jesus tells his disciples at the last supper, *"Do not let your hearts be troubled. Trust in God; trust also in me. In my Father's house are many rooms; if it were not so, I would have told you. I am going there to prepare a place for you. And if I go and prepare a place for you, I will come back and take you to be with me that you may also be where I am going"* (John 14:1-3).

Governments will fail and republics will fall but the promises of God remain steadfast. As we partake of the Lord's Supper we affirm God's covenant, his love for us, and Christ's promise to return and take us back to live with him for eternity. In partaking of the emblems of Christ's body and his blood, we proclaim to all the world that **In God We Trust!**

Let us pray, giving praise to the God in whom we trust...

My How the Colors Change
Revelation 19:13

My, how the colors change! Just a few short weeks ago the trees were a thousand shades of green. But recently other color began creeping in at the edges as if the hem of the green was dipped into it. Then one morning we were awakened early, startled from a slumber, perhaps at the sound of the heavenly paint pots being stored away again. Looking out we saw the green was awash with bright golds and reds, browns and brilliant oranges. As we see the colors splashed across the countryside, we realize God has once again used his power to paint his world beautifully.

My, how the colors change! Now we see lives, perhaps our own, stained a thousand shades of black. Black as sin. For what other color would sin be but black? A black so black it tries to push back the Light. But here, too, is power for change. Revelation says *He is dressed in a robe dipped in blood, and his name is the Word of God (Revelation 19:13).* This color does not creep in, it marches in boldly and says *"Drink...this is my blood of the covenant, which is poured out for many for the forgiveness of sins" (Matthew 26:28).* This color, blood red, covers the black. Not dipped or painted but deeply plunged, our black becomes purest white. This brilliance illuminates the Church in colors so splendid it outdoes the glory of the autumn leaves. We realize that God once again used his power to paint his world beautifully.

In this meal feel his power. Meditate on it, let it enter into your soul and live there, let it wash over the blackness of your sin so that one day you may stand before the Throne of Grace in pure holy whiteness.

Let us pray, giving thanks for changes of color...

In Remembrance of Me...
1 Corinthians 11:23-26

On the communion table in the Calvary United Methodist Church in Dunkirk, Indiana is a big, black, leather-bound pulpit Bible. This Bible was given to the church by Doris Campbell in memory of her husband, Harold, after he passed away in 1966. Some years later, after Mrs. Campbell had moved away from Dunkirk, she returned for a Homecoming celebration with her small grandson. There she pointed out the Bible to the young boy. He saw the gold lettering inside the front cover that read "In Memory of Harold E. Campbell, 1914-1966."

At the same time, the boy saw the communion table carved with the words **"In Remembrance of Me."** He noticed these same words on the communion tables in his own church and in the churches of his friends. For a long time the boy thought it was wonderful that all these churches created memorials for his grandfather and for other people's loved ones.

Later he learned otherwise, but really it is not such a silly idea. For as we gather around the table to partake of the blood and the body of Christ we are partaking together as the Church, the body of Christ. The Church includes not only those who are here now but also those saints who have gone on before us and those yet to come.

And this meal is a special gift to us from Christ. We have received it from the Lord, in remembrance of him, as it has been passed down by those who have come before us. So it is appropriate in remembering Christ to also remember his Church in every age.

*For I received from the Lord what I also pass on to you: The Lord Jesus, on the night he was betrayed, took bread, and when he had given thanks, he broke it and said, "This is my body, which is for you; do this **in remembrance of me.**" The same way, after supper he took the cup, saying, "This cup is the new covenant in my blood; do this whenever you drink it, **in remembrance of me.**" For whenever you eat this bread and drink this cup, you proclaim the Lord's death until he comes (1 Corinthians 11:23-26).*

Let us pray, remembering him...

The Communion of the Saints
Luke 22:30

This week the Christian calendar observed All Saint's Day. But for the most part, All Saint's Day has been forgotten altogether or displaced by Halloween. Halloween is the day set aside for the demons and evil spirits of Satan. On the other hand, All Saint's Day is the day set aside, in Christian tradition, to remember those set apart by God for His own. The term **Saints** refers to the whole company of God's people rather than to any single individual. The primary aspect of sainthood is consecration by God for His service. Thus the Apostle Paul addresses letters to the *saints* in Rome, Ephesus and Phillipi. The obligations and blessings of the Saints are mentioned many times in both the Old and the New Testaments.

This meal of which we are about to partake is sometimes called **the Communion of the Saints.** In this meal we are called to remember Christ's sacrifice on Calvary. But it is also appropriate to remember those Saints of the Church, consecrated and set apart for God's own. As Christ said in Luke 22, *"so that you may eat and drink at my table in my kingdom and sit on thrones judging the twelve tribes of Israel" (Luke 22:30).*

The command "This do in Remembrance of Me, "is also in remembrance of the God of Abraham, Isaac and Jacob, of the God of Luther, Calvin and Zwingli,[10] in remembrance of the God of the Campbells, Stone and Scott,[11] and of the God of *[Ella Mae, Zillah and Ossie.]*[12]

The Lord Jesus, on the night he was betrayed, took bread, and when he had given thanks, he broke it and said, "This is my body, which is for you; do this in remembrance of me. In the same way, after supper he took the cup, saying "This cup is the new covenant in my blood; do this, whenever you drink it, in remembrance of me." For whenever you eat this bread and drink this cup, you proclaim the Lord's death until He comes (I Corinthians 11:23-26).

Let us pray, remembering the saints of the church...

---

10 Leaders of the Sixteenth Century Reformation.
11 Leaders of the Nineteenth Century Reformation, also known as the Restoration Movement.
12 That is Ella Mae Miller, Zillah Taylor, and Ossie Meredith, blessed Saints of the Gap Creek Christian Church, Elizabethton, Tennessee. [The names of saints in the history of your congregation may be substituted here.]

HARK! THE HERALD ANGELS SING
PHILIPPIANS 2:5-8

Charles Wesley and Felix Mendelssohn gave us one of the most beautiful Christmas carols of all time, ***Hark! the Herald Angels Sing***.[13] It is written from the angels' perspective, and they are singing about that first Christmas night, so long ago, when the greatest gift of all time was given. Listen to the second verse:

> *Christ by highest heaven adored;*
> *Christ the everlasting Lord!*
> *Late in time behold him come,*
> *Offspring of the virgin's womb.*
> *Veiled in flesh the God-head see;*
> *Hail th'incarnate Deity,*
> *Pleased as man with men to dwell,*
> *Jesus, our Immanuel.*
> *Hark! the herald angels sing,*
> *"Glory to the new-born King."*

13 Public Domain.

I love those lines "Veiled in flesh the God-head see; Hail th'incarnate Deity." They remind us of the true purpose of Christmas as we enter the season on this first day of Advent. These words remind us this time of year is not about ribbons and bows, paper and packages, twinkling lights and presents under the tree. Instead, this time of year is about God laying his glory by and being born that man no more may die; born to raise the sons of earth, born to give us second birth.

In this season, as we go about our holiday hustle and bustle, each one of us needs to keep as our focus "th'incarnate Deity." Remember his mission was to die at Calvary for the atonement of sins, and remember Christmas is fundamentally about Jesus' obedience to the Father's will. In all you do this season, be obedient to the Father's will in your life. As Paul wrote in Philippians, *Your attitude should be the same as that of Christ Jesus: Who being in very nature God, did not consider equality with God something to be grasped, but made himself nothing, taking on the very nature of servant, being made in human likeness. And being found in appearance as a man, he humbled himself and became obedient to death—even death on cross! (Philippians 2:5-8)*

Let us Hail th'incarnated Deity in prayer...

Light for Those in Darkness
John 1:4-5

Today is the first Sunday of Advent, the season of Christmas. You have probably begun to put up your Christmas decorations, started your shopping and even received a few Christmas cards. If not, those traditional happy activities are sure to pick up in the days ahead. For most of us these days are, as the old song goes, "merry and bright."

Sheila Maxey, a minister of the United Reformed Church in Britain, writes these words about our celebrating and feasting at this time of the year:

"Much as I enjoy the traditional Christmas, I have problems with its relentless cheerfulness: too much light, not enough darkness—and this is where the Gospel accounts of the first Christmas have a clear word to speak. There is much darkness in those stories—a woman in the late stages of pregnancy forced on a long journey by uncaring bureaucracy; no room in the inn; and then fleeing a death threat. The endless light and cheerfulness of the traditional Christmas is not good news to those in darkness. They need to know God came down, a helpless baby, into such a world as theirs."[14]

Those of us in darkness, whether by sin or by circumstance, need to know that behind the temporary glitter of the traditional Christmas we can find the un-flickering message of the Light of the World. *The light shines in the darkness,* wrote the Apostle John, *but the darkness has not understood it.*[15] When we gather around this table, when we partake of these elements, we affirm that *...in him was life, and that life was the light of men.*[16] We throw that light against the darkness and we proclaim, "*Love came down at Christmas*—and stayed."

Let us pray for those in darkness....

---

14 Sheila Maxey, editorial, *Reform,* December 2006, p 3.
15 John 1:5
16 John 1:4

JESUS CHRIST: THE BREAD OF LIFE
LUKE 2:4, 2:7; ISAIAH 1:3

So Joseph also went up from...Galilee to Judea, to Bethlehem, the town of David, because he belonged to the house and the line of David (Luke 2:4). In Hebrew "Bethlehem" comes from the words *beth,* meaning house, and *lehem,* meaning bread. So Bethlehem, the City of David, means the house of bread, the place of food and nourishment.

And she gave birth to her firstborn, a son. She wrapped him in cloths and placed him in a manger... (Luke 2:7). A manger is a feeding trough.

The prophet Isaiah says, *The ox knows his master, the donkey his owner's manger, but Israel does not know, my people do not understand (Isaiah 1:3).*

The ox and the donkey, we are told, know where to get their food, their nourishment. But the people of Israel were rebelling against God and did not understand his provision for them.

It is therefore significant, and in fulfillment of prophecy, that the Messiah should be laid in a manger. The one who would nourish the hearts of man was laid in a feeding trough for God's people. David's Son, the Bread of Life, was born in David's City, the house of bread.

While they were eating Jesus took bread, gave thanks, broke it, and gave it to his disciples saying, 'Take and eat; this is my body' (Matthew 26:26).

The babe lying in the manger in Bethlehem would one day hang on the cross at Golgotha. We come to that cross and to Christ to seek the nourishment that can only come from the assurance of salvation. We are assured of that salvation by this cup poured out and this bread broken for us. [17]

Let us pray, giving thanks for the bread of life...

---

17 First published in the 12 October 1997 issue of Christian Standard.

CLINTON J. HOLLOWAY • LEST WE FORGET

O Little Town of Bethlehem
Micah 5:2

But you, Bethlehem, Ephrathah, though you are small among the clans of Judah, out of you will come for me one who will be ruler over Israel, whose origins are from old, from ancient times (Micah 5:2).

God spoke through the prophet Micah and foretold the judgment against Jerusalem and Samaria caused by Jacob's transgression and the sins of the house of Israel (Micah 1:5). But God is just and does not judge without also offering redemption. That redemption, Micah tells us, would come through the little town of Bethlehem.

O little town of Bethlehem, how still we see thee lie!
Above thy deep and dreamless sleep The silent stars go by;
Yet in thy dark streets shineth The everlasting light:
The hopes and fears of all the years Are met in thee tonight.[18]

Bethlehem was a dusty village, lowly and off the beaten path. Instead of being heralded as the coming Messiah and King from the Temple in Jerusalem, Jesus was born in this quiet place, ushered into

18 *O Little Town of Bethlehem,* Phillips Brooks and Lewis H. Redner, Public Domain.

the world by way of a manger with little pomp and circumstance.

God did not choose these humble circumstances by accident. Had he come by way of a pretentious palace and princely power, few of us could ever be worthy enough to meet him there. But we can all come to the stable and meet him at the unassuming feed box or at the roughly-hewn Roman cross.

How silently, how silently, The wondrous gift is given!
So God imparts to human hearts The blessings of His heaven.
No ear may hear His coming, But in this world of sin,
Where meek souls will receive Him still, the dear Christ enters in.

The prophecy of his coming and his birth in Bethlehem are only the beginning of the story. And we must not think of his death as the end. The story is not finished on the cross. Each time a sinner repents of transgressions, each time we gather around the table to remember, each time we partake of the body and the blood of our Redeemer, the story goes on. The story foretold since ancient of days will not come to an end until he comes again, to take us home. Until then, he abides with us still, as Emmanuel, God with us!

O holy Child of Bethlehem! Descend to us, we pray:
Cast out our sin and enter in, be born in us today.
We hear the Christmas angels The great glad tidings tell;
O come to us, abide with us, Our Lord Emmanuel!

Let us pray to the child of Bethlehem...

FIT US FOR HEAVEN...
PHILIPPIANS 2:6-8

Be near me Lord Jesus!
I ask Thee to stay
Close by me forever,
and love me, I pray.
Bless all the dear children
in Thy tender care,
and fit us for heaven,
to live with Thee there.

These words, the third stanza of *Away in a Manger,* were written over a century ago by John Thomas McFarland.[19] Though the words are old and are typically sung only at Christmastime, they are timeless in their meaning and their message.

They begin with a child-like petition to be wrapped in God's protective embrace: *Be near me Lord Jesus! I ask Thee to stay Close by me forever, and love me, I pray.* The next line calls us to remember our place as his children and asks for his good bounty: *Bless all the dear children in Thy tender care.* The third line

19 Public Domain

understands man's brokenness and inability to achieve salvation on his own. It begs: ***fit us for heaven,*** *to live with Thee there.*

And so he did. There was only one way we could be made fit enough for heaven to live with him there. So Jesus Christ...

Who, being in the very nature God, did not consider equality with God something to be grasped, but made himself nothing, taking the very nature of a servant, being made in human likeness. And being found in appearance as a man, he humbled himself and became obedient to death—even death on a cross! (Philippians 2:6-8).

Let us pray, asking to be made fit for heaven...

THE PERFECT CHRISTMAS TREE
ACTS 5:30-32

Thanksgiving has now passed and until December 25 it seems every moment will be consumed with Christmas preparations: gifts, hundreds of tiny lights to decorate our homes, special meals, parties, and of course the perfect Christmas tree.

What should the perfect Christmas tree look like? The perfect tree should stand straight and tall. Its branches should be exactly even. As for decoration, special ornaments should be placed carefully and evenly on the branches. And an angel or star should "top it off." The tree should also occupy a place of prominence.

Now, let me tell you about the **first Christmas tree**. It too, was a perfect tree. You can bet it was straight and tall; it pointed straight up to heaven. The first Christmas tree had even branches; though there were only two, they were precisely even. As for special decorations, there was really only one. It was beautiful the way it was streaked with crimson. But it was not placed carefully—it was hung crassly, hideously nailed in place. And as for the topper? It was a board reading, *This is the King of the Jews (Luke 23:38).*

This is **the perfect Christmas tree**. This was the *first* Christmas tree. This tree stood prominently on the top of Mount Calvary.

In the book of Acts Peter says, *the God of our fathers raised Jesus from the dead—whom you had killed by hanging him on a tree. God exalted him to his own right hand as Prince and Savior that he might give repentance and forgiveness of sins to Israel. We are witnesses of these things, and so is the Holy Spirit, whom God has given to those who obey him (Acts 5:30-32).*

In this quiet moment, and throughout the busy season, remember with me the significance of this first Christmas tree.

Let us pray, giving witness of these things...

God With Us
Isaiah 7:14

Moses first foretold his birth in the book of Genesis when God promised Abraham descendants as numerous as the stars. But his name would not be given until much later. It is recorded in the book of Isaiah, *Therefore the Lord himself shall give you a sign; Behold, a virgin shall conceive, and bear a son, and shall call his name Immanuel (Isaiah 7:14; KJV).*

The book of Matthew again records this prophecy but adds the meaning of the name Immanuel: **God with us.** There is assurance in that name. Notice there is no adverb qualifying the verb. Immanuel means **God with us.** It does not mean God *was* with us, in the past, or God *will be* with us, in the future. That would mean somehow there was a beginning or an end of God's presence among us. Instead, before us, He Was; and after us, He Will Yet Be.

One of our favorite Christmas hymns is an adapted ninth-century plainsong, *O Come, O Come Emmanuel.* The first verse reads:

O Come, O Come Emmanuel,
And ransom captive Israel,

That mourns in lonely exile here,
Until the Son of God appear.
Rejoice! Rejoice! Emmanuel
Shall come to thee, O Israel![20]

Although we are captive to sin, the song bids us to be happy for **God with us** shall come, and did come, and he will come again. The assurance that he is with us is never clearer than when we partake of the elements representing his body and blood. *For whenever you eat this bread and drink this cup, you proclaim the Lord's death until he comes.*

Let us pray to God with us...

---

20 The origins of this song date back as early as the 9th Century. The first verse is traditionally attributed to John M. Neale, Public Domain.

EBENEZER

1 SAMUEL 7:12

In the days of the judgment of Samuel the hand of the Lord went out against the Philistines on behalf of the people of Israel. The Lord thundered against them and the Philistines were routed before the Israelites. *Then Samuel took a stone, and set it between Mizpah and Shen, and called the name of it Ebenezer, saying Hitherto hath the Lord helped us (I Samuel 7:12; KJV).*

Ebenezer is a Hebrew word meaning "stone of help." Samuel set up a stone of help to remind the people of Israel the *Lord* had defeated the Philistines. In passing by the ebenezer they remembered not only "Hitherto hath the Lord helped us" but also that his help would continue beyond that point.

Today stands as an ebenezer for the *[Gap Creek Christian Church.]*[21] Today is not a day to simply remember the past or to dwell on what once was. No, today stands as an ebenezer to remind those of us assembled here, and to stand witness to the rest of the world, that "Hitherto hath the Lord helped us."

Communion is also an ebenezer, a stone of help. For by this stone Christ calls the world to remember his death and burial in

———⊗⊗⊗———

21 [The name and founding date of your congregation should be inserted here.]

the past, the continuing significance of his resurrection and the future hope of his return. Hitherto the Lord has helped us—and each time we partake of this ebenezer, we remember his resurrection and the promise of his continual help.

The Lord Jesus, on the night he was betrayed, took bread, and when he had given thanks, he broke it and said, "This is my body, which is for you; do this in remembrance of me." The same way, after supper he took the cup, saying, "This cup is the new covenant in my blood, do this, whenever you drink it, in remembrance of me." For whenever you eat this bread and drink this cup, you proclaim the Lord's death until he comes (I Corinthians 11:23b-26).

Let us pray, remembering our stone of help...

The Call of a Life Recruit
Selections from Romans

Would you want to pay God's phone bill? Have you ever noticed he is always calling somebody to do something? You could think of the Bible as God's itemized phone bill. For example, let us look at the Book of Romans:

1:1 Paul, a servant of Jesus Christ, **called** to be an apostle...

1:6 and you also are among those who are **called** to belong to Jesus Christ...

1:7 To all in Rome who are loved by God and **called** to be saints...

8:28 And we know that in all things God works for the good of those who love him, who have been **called** according to his purpose...

11:29 For God's gifts and his **call** are irrevocable...

A calling from God can come in so many ways: we are called to worship, called to make disciples, called to go forth, we have altar calls and we go calling. But one thing we know from his word—we are called according to his purpose. We are called to serve him with our entire life. Today we come together to send out one who is giving his life to that calling. I would like to share with you a poem that speaks to this calling.

The Call of a Life Recruit

When evening shadows cross the sun,

The twilight winds do tenderly

Call for a life. Yet it is none

But God, and He is calling me.

In stillness of the evening air

The myriad angels earnestly

Call sweet and clear. Yet none is there

But Christ, and He is calling me.

I hear the trees at close of day,

And often, often turn to see

The one who bids me serve, But nay,

'Tis but the Spirit's call to me.

But when life's race at last is run,

And I am called across the sea;

When I can hear the word "well done,"

I'll know the voice that called to me.[22]

At this time we are also called to a very specific purpose. At the

22 Poem by Dr. Elmer Lewis, former President of Milligan College (Tennessee).

Last Supper Jesus called together his twelve apostles so they might partake before being sent out. Jesus calls us, as well, to partake of this memorial meal and to proclaim his death until he comes again.

Let us pray to the one who calls us...

Make this Last Meal One to Remember
John 6:35

When Jesus' disciples gathered in that upper room on the day of the Feast of Unleavened Bread they did not know it would be their last day together, and their last meal as a group. But Christ was certainly aware this was the very last time that they would gather around the table as a "family" to laugh, to share, and to eat with one another.

Jesus intended to make this last meal one to remember. With this meal Jesus wanted to say something special to his followers. He wanted to give them a way to remember his promises. He wanted to remind them and reassure them he would come again. He wanted them—and he wanted us—to remember he is the Bread of Life, that those who come to him will never go hungry and those who believe in him will never be thirsty (John 6:35).

The Lord Jesus, on the night he was betrayed, took bread, and when he had given thanks, he broke it and said, "This is my body, which is for you; do this in remembrance of me." The same way, after supper he took the cup, saying, "This cup is the new covenant in my blood; do this whenever you drink it, in remembrance of me." For whenever you eat this bread and drink this cup, you proclaim he Lord's death until he comes (I Corinthians 11: 23b-26).

Let us pray that this last meal will be one to remember...

FORGETTING WHAT IS BEHIND...
STRAINING TOWARD WHAT IS AHEAD
PHILIPPIANS 3:10-16; 20-21

Sometimes we forget why we are here. In times of struggle, anxiety, and doubt, through seasons of discord and dark periods of introspection, we can really question why we are part of the church. But there are other times: at the deathbed of a church member, celebrating the birth of a child, gathering around this Table—at these times, which one author calls "patches of God light," we can remember why we are here. These times remind us that *people* are the church, the body of Christ.

Chances are many of you have had similar thoughts. I think even the greatest followers of Christ had the same questions. Look at Paul: beaten, abused, threatened, arrested, chained to a Roman guard. Paul was under house arrest while he wrote Philippians. In chapter 3 Paul warns the Philippians to be careful of things that would steal their joy and turn them from their true calling; things that might cause them to quit the race before attaining the prize. Paul encourages them with these words of his own testimony:

I want to know Christ and the power of his resurrection and the fellowship of sharing in his sufferings, becoming like him in his death, and so, somehow to attain to the resurrection from the dead. Not that I have already obtained all this—or have already been made perfect—but I press on to take hold of that for which Jesus Christ took hold of me. Brothers, I do not consider myself yet to have taken hold of it. But one thing I do: **(Listen up here, folks!)** *Forgetting what is behind and straining toward what is ahead, I press on toward the goal to win the prize for which God has called me heavenward in Christ Jesus. All of us who are mature should take such a view of things. And if on some point you think differently that too God will make clear to you. Only let us live up to what we have already attained.* **Dropping down to verse 20.** *(But) our citizenship is in heaven. And we eagerly await a Savior from there, the Lord Jesus Christ, who by the power that enables him to bring everything under his control will transform our lowly bodies so that they will be like his glorious body (Philippians 3:10-16; 20-21).*

Some may think that this is a sad day because it's the last day we will worship in this building. While this building has represented the faith, generosity and hard work of many people for many years, we should not let brick and mortar, or suffering, or anxiety, or any other circumstance keep us from pressing on toward the goal which God himself has called us heavenward.

When we gather for worship, whether it be in this building or in some other or in no building at all, we have the opportunity to forget what is behind and strain toward what is ahead by remembering the broken body and shed blood of Jesus. For whenever *(and wherever!)* you eat this bread and drink this cup, you proclaim the Lord's death until he comes.

Let us pray: Father, help us to forget what is behind and strain towards what is ahead...

SUITABLE FOR ANY OCCASION

The Body Re-membered
1 Corinthians 11:24b-25

The Church is the body of Christ on Earth. But that Church, like the physical body of Christ as it hung upon the tree, is broken. The body is torn apart by denominationalism, differences of opinion, and bad doctrine. Petty grievances have divided blessed fellowship among believers for centuries. Even we, the "Restoration Movement," who have called people together under the flag of "unity" are now divided into at least three major branches. One author calls this broken body "the Shattered Cross." If we are the body, then we are **dis-membered**; torn apart.

But in this supper we are called to **re-member;** to come back together in remembrance of Him. We are most whole as the body of Christ on Earth when we gather around this table, because at this moment we join with Christians all over the globe, whatever their denomination, differences or doctrine; we join them in re-membering the sacrifice of Jesus Christ. It is at this table that we come back together, re-membering the body of Christ.

And when he had given thanks, he broke it, and said Take, eat: this is my body, which is broken for you: this do in remembrance of me. After the same manner also he took the cup...saying, this cup

is the new testament in my blood: this do ye, as oft as ye drink it,
in remembrance of me (I Corinthians 11:24b-25; KJV).

Let us pray, re-membering the body of Christ....

So This Isn't Home Sweet Home...Adjust!
John 14:1-4

There is a cross-stitched sampler that reads, **"SO THIS ISN'T HOME SWEET HOME...ADJUST."** Obviously, the creator of this piece not only had a sense of humor, but an understanding of our world. As Christians this terrestrial ball we call Earth is not our home. We may live here for our allotted three score and ten years but this is **only** a waiting place; we are only passing through.

The Gospel of John records these words of Christ at the Last Supper: *"Do not let your hearts be troubled. Trust in God; trust also in me. In my Father's house there are many rooms; if it were not so, I would have told you. I am going there to prepare a place for you. And if I go and prepare a place for you, I will come back and take you to be with me that you may also be where I am. You know the way to the place where I am going" (John 14:1-4).*

Jesus is going to His Father's house, in Heaven. Paradise. For eternity. He has prepared this place for you and me by his death on Calvary's tree. He is there now appearing before God on behalf of his people. As we come to this table and partake of the emblems representing the body and the blood, we are reminded that this is not our home. Our home is in heaven and we must be continually **adjusting** our life to one of more perfect communion with the one who has made us...bought us...and who is preparing a place for us to live with him...for eternity.

The Lord Jesus, on the night he was betrayed, took bread, and when he had given thanks, he broke it and said "this is my body, which is broken for you; do this in remembrance of me." The same way, after supper, he took the cup saying, "This is the new covenant in my blood; do this, whenever you drink it, in remembrance of me." For whenever you eat this bread and drink this cup you proclaim the Lord's death until he comes (1 Corinthians 11 23b-26).

Let us pray, adjusting our heart, mind, and soul toward home...

That is the Most Beautiful Thing
I Have Ever Seen!
Acts 7:54-56

In the seventh chapter of Acts we find Stephen preaching before the Sanhedrin. The Jewish leaders of the Sanhedrin considered Stephen's testimony to be blasphemy. They particularly resisted his claim of having seen Heaven open up and of seeing Christ standing beside the Father. Remember, this was the Christ the Sanhedrin had sought to kill.

When they heard this, they were furious and gnashed their teeth at him. But Stephen, full of the Holy Spirit, looked up to Heaven and saw the glory of God. "Look," he said, "I see Heaven open and the Son of Man standing at the right hand of God" (Acts 7:54-56).

Stephen seeing the glory of the Father just before death has been likened to the stories of people having visions of Heaven just before they crossed to the other side. Ralph Starr,[23] a faithful Indiana farmer, had one of those visions. As he lay in the hospital bed, his legs amputated due to extreme hardening of the arteries, his life ebbing away, he looked toward the foot of his bed where there was nothing anyone else could see. He said, **"That is the most**

---

23 Ralph Starr was a paternal great-grandfather of the author.

beautiful thing I have ever seen!" He laid his head back on his pillow and he was gone.

When we gather around this table, to partake of this meal, we should see the Heavens rolled back like a scroll, and we should see Christ standing at the right hand of God. We should see the nail prints in his hands and feet, his pierced side, the stripes upon his back. These wounds should make us shudder in pain but they should also cause us to say, **"That is the most beautiful thing I have ever seen!"** These wounds paid our ransom of sin and guarantee eternal life to all believers.

The Lord Jesus, on the night he was betrayed, took bread, and when he had given thanks, he broke it and said, "This is my body, which is for you; do this in remembrance of me." The same way, after supper, He took the cup, saying, "This cup is the new covenant in my blood; do this, whenever you drink it, in remembrance of me." For whenever you eat this bread and drink this cup, you proclaim the Lord's death until he comes (1 Corinthians 11:23b-26).

Let us pray with the vision in our eyes of the most beautiful thing we will ever see...

Joseph Paid for His Body That Day
Mark 15:43; John 6:51-54

At the time of Jesus' crucifixion, Roman custom refused to allow the body of executed criminals to be buried. The victims of crucifixion were often left on their crosses as a deterrent against further criminal activity. This custom was particularly appalling to the Jews who believed the soul was in jeopardy without proper burial of the physical body.

Among the members of the Sanhedrin, the great Jewish council which condemned Jesus to death, at least two Jews disagreed with the decision. One was Nicodemus, the other a man named Joseph, from the Judean village of Arimathea. Both were secret disciples of Jesus.

Jesus had been executed as a criminal, the leader in a rebellion against Rome. So in asking for the body, Joseph of Arimathea might have been implicated in treason. But Joseph went **boldly** to Pilate to ask for Christ's body so it might have an honorable burial (Mark 15:43). Tradition says **Joseph *paid* for His body that day,** then took it to his own new tomb for burial. Nicodemus brought 75 pounds of myrrh and aloe to anoint the body. They wrapped the body in a linen shroud and laid a great stone before the entrance to the cave to further protect the body of Christ.

Oh, that we should have such reverence for the crucified and risen body of our Lord Jesus Christ, through which believers are guaranteed eternal life! The broken body of Christ is symbolized here by the broken bread.

In the sixth chapter of John, Jesus says, *"I am the living bread that came down from heaven. If anyone eats of this bread, he will live forever. This bread is my flesh, which I will give for the life of the world."*

Then the Jews began to argue sharply amongst themselves, "How can this man give us his flesh to eat?"

Jesus said to them "I tell you the truth, unless you eat the flesh of the Son of Man and drink his blood, you have no life in you. Whoever eats my flesh and drinks my blood has eternal life, and I will raise him up at the last day" (John 6:51-54).

Let us pray with reverence for the broken body of our risen Lord...

SACRAMENTUM
1 CORINTHIANS 11:23B-26

The Christian faith has many names for this gathering around the table: the Lord's Supper, the Breaking of the Bread, Holy Communion, the *Communio Sanctorum (koh-MOO-nee-oh sonk-TOH-rum)*, or the Communion of Saints. Some faiths call it an ordinance, others a sacrament. They are both correct, but it is this last definition, **sacrament**, I wish to focus on today.

Before his enrollment in the Roman army, a new recruit had to swear an oath of loyalty to Caesar. This oath was his ***sacramentum (sah-krah-MEN-tum)***, the Latin word from which we get our English word "sacrament." The sacramentum or oath of loyalty had to be renewed on a yearly basis. It was an outward expression of faith in and loyalty to the Roman Caesar.

The first century Christians would have been familiar with this custom given their frequent contact with the Roman Army. So it was natural for the early church to adopt a known word for the new custom instituted by Christ in the breaking of the bread. The Lord's Supper is an outward expression of faith and fellowship with the risen Christ and his people. And while the Roman soldier renewed his oath of loyalty each year, we are called to affirm our "oath" to the new covenant with Christ *"as oft as ye drink it."*

The Lord Jesus on the night he was betrayed, took bread, and when he had given thanks, he broke it, and said "This is my body, which is for you; do this in remembrance of me." The same way after supper he took the cup saying "This cup is the new covenant in my blood; do this whenever you drink it, in remembrance of me." For whenever you eat this bread and drink this cup, you proclaim the Lord's death until he comes (1 Corinthians 11: 23b-26).

Let us pray, swearing our allegiance to the one true King...

Trivial Pursuit
Matthew 19:16, 18b-22

My favorite game, largely because it's one of the few games I am good at, is **Trivial Pursuit.**[24] Knowing details and facts, rather than possessing skill or talent, is the key to playing the game. So there is a Biblical figure I can relate to one who wanted to know the details and facts of Christian life.

Now a man came up to Jesus and asked, "Teacher, what good thing must I do to get eternal life?"

...Jesus replied "Do not murder, do not commit adultery, do not steal, do not give false testimony, honor your father and your mother, and 'love your neighbor as yourself."

"All of these I have kept" the young man said. "What do I still lack?"

Jesus answered, "If you want to be perfect, go, sell your possessions and give to the poor and you will have treasure in heaven. Then come, follow me."

When the young man heard this he went away sad because he had great wealth (Matthew 19:16, 18b-22).

---

24 Trivial Pursuit is a registered trademark of Horn Abbot Ltd. And Horn Abbot International Limited.

The Rich Young Man was not interested in serving or in discipleship. He wanted the details, but lost interest when the stakes of the game became too high. He was not interested in truly following Christ; the Rich Young Man was interested only in the **Trivial Pursuit.**

As we come around the Table of the Lord let the meditations of our hearts and the actions of our lives be not on the less important details but on the focus of following the lamb of Christ who makes us perfect through his blood shed on Calvary.

For whenever you eat this bread and drink this cup, you proclaim the Lord's death until He comes (I Corinthians 11:26).

Let us pray, laying aside all trivial pursuits...

He Wasted His Substance in Riotous Living
Luke 15:11-13

In his Gospel, Luke records the Parable of the Lost Son. The King James Version calls him the Prodigal Son; I prefer the way this version tells the story.

And he said, "A certain man had two sons: and the younger of them said to his father, Father, give me the portion of goods that falleth to me. And he divided unto them his living. And not many days after the younger son gathered all together, and took his journey into a far country, and there **he wasted his substance with riotous living**" *(Luke 15:11-13).*

Many teachers will translate the meaning of "his substance" as being his wealth; that he spent all of his money. While this is true, the implications can be so much more. Not only did the younger son foolishly waste his money, but he forsook his family, his homeland, and his God. He lost control of himself in the drinking halls, he lost his pride in the gambling dens, and he lost his purity in the houses of ill-repute. When he wasted his substance he wasted much more than his money; he wasted significant parts of himself.

After this the younger son was forced to feed with the hogs. Then Luke says, "When he came to his senses he remembered his father!" At once he traveled toward home, and while he was still a long way off his father saw him, ran to him, and threw wide open his forgiving arms.

When Christ told this parable he knew we were the sons and daughters who have **"wasted our substance in riotous living."** But when we come to our senses and remember our Father, *we can reclaim our lost substance.* While we were still a long way off, Jesus also threw wide open his forgiving arms...and had them nailed opened on the tree of Calvary.

While they were eating, Jesus took bread, gave thanks and broke it, and gave it to his disciples saying "Take and eat; this is my body."

Then he took the cup, gave thanks and offered it to them saying, "Drink from it, all of you. This is the blood of the covenant which is poured out for many for the forgiveness of sins" (Matthew 26:26-28).

Let us pray, asking that our substance be restored through Christ Jesus...

Lord, is it I?
Matthew 26:21-25

And as they did eat, he said, Verily I say unto you, that one of you shall betray me.

And they were exceeding sorrowful, and began every one of them to say unto him, Lord, is it I?

And he answered and said, He that dippeth his hand with me in the dish, the same shall betray me. The Son of Man goeth as it is written of him, but woe unto the man by whom the Son of Man is betrayed! it had been good for that man if he had not been born.

Then Judas, which betrayed him, answered and said, Master, is it I?

He said unto him, Thou hast said (Matthew 26:21-25; KJV).

Jesus was very direct in pointing out his betrayer. When Judas asked, "Master, is it I?" he answered his own question and convicted himself. He knew he was the betrayer. The thirty pieces of silver weighed heavy in his pocket to remind him.

But as we come to the table let us not be too hasty in judging Judas. He was not the only follower who forsook the Messiah that night. John slept, Peter denied him three times, and then all the disciples deserted him and fled.

And what about you and me? Should we not also ask, "Lord, is it I?" Have we not also betrayed him by our sin? This table stands here to remind us and to convict us of our sin. But it is also the place we can partake of the blood of the covenant, which "is poured out for many for the forgiveness of sin." We must ask "Lord, is it I?" knowing that our very question convicts us. But his forgiving answer to us is "YES! **BUT** go-and sin no more!"

Let us pray, knowing that it is *I* who sins but it is *He* who forgives...

Sponsored bei Oma
Luke 24

There was a German youth whose *Oma (OH-mah)*,[25] or Grandma, bought him an automobile, his first car. It was a gift of love and a sacrifice for Oma to buy this car. In honor of her gift, to remember her gift, and so others would recognize the gift, he put a bumper sticker on his car that read **"Sponsored bei Oma"** *(sponsored by OH-mah)*. In other words, "Paid for by Grandma."

In the twenty-fourth chapter of Luke we find two disciples on the road to Emmaus after the resurrection. Jesus joined them but we are told they were kept from recognizing him (verse 16). When they arrived in Emmaus the disciples urged Jesus to stay with them, which he did (verse 29). It was not until he was seated at the table with them and he had taken the bread, given thanks for it, broken it, and began to give it to them that their eyes were opened and they recognized him (verse 31).

The meal that is laid before us is sponsored by Christ. He has made the invitation. This is our weekly opportunity to consciously remember Christ and his sacrifice. We are, like the disciples of Emmaus, able to most recognize Christ in the breaking of the bread.

─────❈─────

25 Oma is the German word for Grandma.

While they were eating, Jesus took bread, gave thanks and broke it, and gave it to his disciples, saying, "Take and eat; this is my body."

Then he took the cup, gave thanks and offered it to them, saying, "Drink from it, all of you. This is my blood of the covenant, which is poured out for many for the forgiveness of sins" (Matthew 26:26-28).

Let us pray, remembering the sponsor and host of this meal...

Yours to Count On...
John 14:2-3

The Gospel of John records this promise of Christ at the Last Supper: *"In my Father's house there are many rooms; if it were not so, I would have told you. I am going there to prepare a place for you. And if I go and prepare a place for you, I will come back and take you to be with me that you may also be where I am"* *(John 14:2-3).*

In the Shenandoah Valley, there stands a stately antebellum mansion, you know the kind, with the tall imposing pillars out front. In one room of that mansion hangs a painting of the great Confederate General J.E.B. Stuart. It is said this painting was the personal gift of the General to the family who lived in the house. And if you look closely, down in the corner of the painting, it is signed "**Yours to count on, J.E.B. Stuart.**"

This sacrificial meal is a personal gift to us, the family of God, and reminds us one day he <u>will</u> come back for us. Take a close look at this meal—down in the corner, it is signed in blood "**Yours to count on, Jesus Christ.**"

For whenever you eat this bread and drink this cup, you proclaim the Lord's death until he comes (I Corinthians 11:26).

Let us pray, remembering the sacrifice of the only one we can truly count on...

Picture It
John 6:51

Close your eyes and imagine Jesus. In our minds, we each picture Christ in different ways, and we see him in relationship to ourselves, based on our experiences and worldview. For instance, those suffering under oppression may see Christ as Liberator. Slaves would understand the imagery of Christ as Lord and Master. Some will picture Christ as the humble servant bending to wash the feet of his disciples. Others want to think of Christ riding a shining white horse, with flags flying and trumpets sounding; this is Christ as the Victor over Evil. And do you know that each of these pictures of Christ is correct? He is our Liberator from bondage, the Master whom we serve, the Servant who is our help, and the Victory over Death.

Other influences on the way we picture Jesus are the artistic representations we have seen in scuplture, in painting, and in word. For many of us who grew up in North American churches in the last half of the twentieth century, one of our favorite pictures is the familiar painting by Warner Sallman of the head and shoulders of Christ.[26] It is painted in beautiful browns and golds,

———————

26 *Head of Christ,* Warner Sallman, 1941. This portrait and a considerable body of Sallman's work, are jointly owned by Anderson (Indiana) University and Warner Press. *Head of Christ* and others can be seen at www.warnersallman.com

with Jesus' piercing blue eyes looking up from the canvas to his Father in Heaven.

But this picture holds "more than meets the eye." Mr. Sallman used the picture to remind us of Christ's mission, because if you look closely you can see an image of the loaf and cup in the shadows on Christ's forehead.

No matter how we picture Jesus, he is bigger, more gracious, and more loving than we can ever imagine. We must continually expand our picture of him.

On the night he was betrayed, Jesus said, *"I am the living bread that came down from heaven. If anyone eats of this bread, he will live forever. This bread is my flesh, which I will give for the life of the world" (John 6:51).*

Let us pray, picturing Jesus' sacrifice at Calvary...

What Can Wash Away My Sins?
Matthew 26:26-29

I like the story about the two young boys who stood before a baptistery, intently peering into the water. Noticing the sediment that clouded the bottom of the water, the first little boy asked his friend, "What do you suppose it is?" The older and wiser boy says, matter-of-factly, "IT'S SIN!"

How right he is! Not literally, of course. THAT baptistery just needs to be cleaned more often! But he is right in that when we as sinners step into the water and are baptized, we are cleansed of our sins. We rise to a newness of life leaving our sins behind. The blood of Jesus, represented in the baptistery by water and at this table by the fruit of the vine, washes all sin away.

Matthew 26 says, *While they were eating, Jesus took bread, gave thanks and broke it, and gave it to his disciples, saying "Take and eat; this is my body."*

Then he took the cup, gave thanks and offered it to them, saying, "Drink from it, all of you. This is my blood of the new covenant, which is poured out for many for the forgiveness of sins. I tell you, I will not drink of the fruit of the vine from now on until that day when I drink it anew with you in my Father's kingdom" (Matthew 26:26-29).

Let us pray, asking to be washed clean of our sin...

To Me, To Live is Christ
Philippians 1:21

The following thoughts were found among the papers of Edith Taylor Campbell, a woman who lived for Christ well past her ninetieth year. The author is unknown.

When as a child,
I laughed and wept,
Time crept.
When as a youth,
I dreamed and talked,
Time walked.
When I became a full grown man,
Time ran;
When older still I daily grew,
Time flew;
Soon shall I find in traveling on,
Time gone.

One life to live,
'Twill soon be past

Only what's done

For Christ will last.

To me to live is Christ.

This last thought is from Paul's prison epistle to the Philippians. The verse reads, *For to me, to live is Christ and to die is gain (Philippians 1:21).* Paul was torn between a fruitful ministry on earth and his desire to depart from this world and be with Christ. Though he was in chains and it appeared his life was in jeopardy, Paul realized that by himself he was unimportant. It was Christ in him that made his life important and if he was to live, he was to live for Christ. Only what is done for Christ will last.

Like Paul, our lives are given meaning by Christ living in us, by his death on the cross, by his broken body and shed blood commemorated here in the loaf and the cup. As we live our lives make them count by living for Christ. So that "in traveling on" we do not find "time gone."

Let us pray, seeking always to live Christ in our lives...

His Hands
Mark 10:16

What you would remember most about Ralph are his hands. Ralph Mowery was a member of First Christian Church, Bluffton, Indiana.[27] He had lived a long life; probably a retired farmer. Ralph had the biggest hands you have ever seen! They were thick and powerful after a lifetime of manual labor. When he took your hand, and clapped it between his own in a warm and friendly handshake, and spoke to you in that deep, rich voice, you felt the blessing of God. Often he was the first person to begin applauding after a special song or a children's program. When those two mighty hands came together the sound echoed thunderously through the vaulted-ceiling sanctuary. His applause was truly praise to his Creator, not an appeal to a performer's vanity.

Ralph's hands remind us of another set of hands. Hands that flung stars into space, hands that reached into the formless and dark void and created Earth. Hands that reached inside of man and took a rib to form for him a help meet. Hands that parted the waters before Moses and closed them on Pharaoh. Hands that took Elijah to heaven in a whirlwind and called forth Lazarus

---

27 The congregation where the author grew up.

from among the dead. Hands that rebuked and were raised in anger against those who had turned his Father's house into a den of thieves. Hands that also comforted and healed. I am reminded of hands that surrendered to the nails.

The Gospel of Mark tells the story of Jesus and the little children. Parents brought their little ones to Jesus so he could touch them, but the disciples rebuked the parents. Verse 16 of chapter 10 tells us, *And he took the children in his arms, put his hands on them and blessed them.* By the touch of the Master's hand the children received a blessing! We are also his children. And by those hands, we also have received a blessing. In this memorial meal we again are reminded that Christ has his arms open wide, ready to receive us, to lay his hands on us and bless us. His hands have done all the work, and all we need to do is believe in the touch of the Master's nail scarred hands.

Let us pray, remembering his hands...

Families: Born and Made
Romans 8:22-25

Families are a curious thing. We can take enormous pride in our family or be mortified of our relationship to "Cousin Black Sheep." We have no control over the family we are born into, and sometimes it hurts to be part of our family. We envy those who appear to have the "perfect family."

[I am fortunate to be born into proud families with long recorded genealogies. I am one of the Campbells, the Journays, the Starrs and the Holloways. I am a descendant from the Biblers, the Keans, the Stewarts and the Ulmers.][28] The farther back I go the more family lines there are, all of which come down through my grandparents and parents to me. These are the families I was born into.

But there are also families that are made. When you marry, you marry "the one" but you get the lot—sometimes whether you like it or not! There are friends who stick closer than a brother. Sometimes a close knit college community will refer to themselves as a college "family." We often speak of our congregation as our "church family." In worship we might sing about being glad

---

28 The reader's family history and family names may be substituted here.

to be a part of the family of God. There may be many groups in our lifetime for which we come to feel the familial bond. In all of these families we choose to be a part. We take great pride in these families and eagerly anticipate being with them. We are adopted into them and welcomed as a full-fledged member.

In the book of Romans, Paul writes about our adoption into the family of Christ: *We know that the whole creation has been groaning as in the pains of childbirth right up to the present time. Not only so, but we ourselves, who have the first fruits of the Spirit, groan inwardly as we eagerly wait for our adoption as sons, the redemption of our bodies. For in this hope we are saved. But hope that is seen is no hope at all. Who hopes for what he already has? But if we hope for what we do not yet have, we wait for it patiently (Romans 8:22-25).*

We are saved in this hope of redemption, in this hope of adoption as sons and daughters of the loving Father, through the sacrifice of the Son. Through this hope we become part of the largest family ever with roots tracing back thousands of years. We look forward to that glorious family reunion, when we will at last be taken up, and will live together with our brothers and sisters and with the Father and the Son for eternity. Just now, as the family gathered in this place, let us anticipate the feast for which we hope and wait.

Let us pray to our Father, giving thanks for families born and made...

Keep Your Eyes on Christ!
Hebrews 12:2

A famous radio minister tells of a time when he was struggling with a great deal of opposition as a young preacher. In the midst of the turmoil, an elderly member of his church invited him to her apartment for lunch. He hesitated because he was busy and did not want to listen to what he anticipated to be her lecture, but he finally agreed.

He met her downstairs at the retirement community where she lived. They had a delightful lunch together, and then she explained there was something she wanted to show him in her apartment. She took him to a picture hanging on her living room wall, a picture of Daniel in the lion's den. "Son," she said, "look at this picture and tell me what you see."

The young preacher looked at the picture and saw all the lions had their mouths closed. Some were lying down and some were standing. Daniel was standing with his hands behind him, looking up at the ray of light coming into the den. He pointed out every detail he could see. "Is there anything else?" she asked.

He could think of nothing. She put her arm on his shoulder and said, "Son, what I want you to see is that Daniel does not have his eyes on the lions; he has his eyes on Christ."

The author of Hebrews says, *Let us fix our eyes on Jesus, the author and perfector of our faith, who for the joy set before him endured the cross, scorning its shame, and sat down at the right hand of the throne of God (Hebrews 12:2).*

As we partake of the Lord's Supper let us be reminded not to let our focus fall on the everyday cares of this world, the concerns that threaten us at every turn. Instead, let's keep our eyes on Christ, the author and perfector of our faith, who endured the cross and its shame so that we too, may sit with him at the right hand of throne of God.

Let us pray, keeping our eyes fixed on Christ...

Accidentally Versus Intentionally
Matthew 26:28

I want to point out a mistake we often make. Oh, I think I am guilty of it, too. You see, we say it accidentally. I do not believe our theological misstatement is intentional.

So many times when we gather around the Table to partake of the body and the blood of our risen Lord, we talk about his blood that was "spilled" for us. But these words are a mistake. Jesus' blood was not spilled. The word "spilled" implies the action was done without an intended purpose in mind, as in "spilled milk. "Spilled" means the act was accidental, not intentional. In all of the scriptures spilled is used only a few times and never in relation to Jesus.

The words we should use are *"poured out."* More than fifty times the scriptures use the phrase "poured out." According to modern translations these are the words Jesus himself used. "Poured out" tells us the act was not accidental but intentional. It was done with meaning and with purpose and that purpose is the forgiveness and remission of sins.

While they were eating, Jesus took bread gave thanks and broke it, and gave it to the disciples, saying, "Take and eat; this is my body."

*Then he took the cup, gave thanks and offered it to them, saying, "Drink from it, all of you. This is my blood of the covenant, which is **poured out** for many for the forgiveness of sins"(Matthew 26:26-28).*

Let us pray, giving thanks for the blood that was intentionally poured out...

BETWEEN ME AND THEE
HEBREWS 9:11-14

In the old Tabernacle and Temple a veil separated the Most Holy Place, the place where God dwelled, from the outer courts. Both symbolically and in reality this veil separated God from everybody else. The veil, or curtain, as we find in Exodus, was made of... *blue, purple, and scarlet yarn and finely twisted linen, with cherubim worked into it by skilled craftsman (Exodus 26:31).* But more than the curtain, the sin and uncleanness of the people separated them from the Holy of Holies.

At the moment of Christ's death, the Gospels tell us the curtain was torn in two, **from top to bottom,** for the first time giving all people free and direct access to God. Though we now have this complete and unhindered access to God, we insist on restoring that curtain between us. Our curtain is not made of scarlet yarn and finely twisted linen. Rather, our curtain is made of the blackest and most severely twisted sin. Yes, there is still a veil between God and man, a curtain made of our own sin.

Hebrews 9:11-14 says, *When Christ came as high priest of the good things that are already here, he went through the greater and more perfect tabernacle that is not man-made, that is to say, not a part of this creation. He did not enter be means of the blood of goats and calves; but he entered the Most Holy Place once for all by his own blood, having obtained eternal redemption. The blood of goats and bulls and the ashes of a heifer sprinkled on those who are ceremonially unclean sanctify them so that they are outwardly clean. How much more, then, will the blood of Christ, who through the eternal Spirit offered himself unblemished to God, cleanse our consciences from acts that lead to death, so that we may serve a living God!*

We are granted to come to this table once again so that by his blood we might be cleansed of sins that lead to death. Let Jesus tear your curtain of sin from top to bottom, let him remove the veil, let him be your access into the Most Holy Place so that you may serve a living God!

Let us pray, seeking that no veil of sin should separate us from God...

I Want *You!*
Acts 13:38-39a

In the thirteenth chapter of Acts, Doctor Luke records these words of Paul: "*Therefore, my brothers, **I want you** to know that through Jesus the forgiveness of sins is proclaimed to you. Through him everyone who believes is justified...*" *(Acts 13:38-39a).*

Do you remember the old recruiting poster of Uncle Sam? There he was, Uncle Sam, dressed in his trademark red, white, and blue. His arm was stretched out with his finger pointing at you, saying "**I Want You!**" I suppose many a young man and woman answered the patriotic call and served our country because of that poster.

But at this moment, with my mind's eye, I am seeing another picture. This picture is not of Uncle Sam, but it is of Jesus. His arm, too, is stretched out, but instead of pointing his finger, he is holding his hand out. I can see the nail print. And he, too, is saying, "**I Want You!**"

Jesus does not call us to serve in any earthly army but to join him in the Lord's army. The army of the Lord is made up of sinners everywhere who have believed in him. They have received his forgiveness through his sacrifice on the tree of Calvary, represented here by the bread and the cup.

Let us pray, giving thanks because he wants us for his kingdom...

AGE DEO FIDE ET AMORE
2 TIMOTHY 1:13-14

There is a Latin motto which says **Age Deo Fide et Amore (AH-gay DAY-oh FEE-day et ah-MOR-ay).**[29] It means "Act for God with Faith and Love." Here *Age* is translated as a second person imperative: You! Thus the motto says, You! act for God with faith and love. It is a command to each and every one of us to conduct our lives as servant-children of God. This lifestyle requires faith in God to do what He has said He would do, and love for God as He has first loved us. Faith and love are to be the guiding forces motivating our every action.

The Apostle Paul, in writing his second epistle to his son in the faith, Timothy, cautioned him to remember the faith and love. *What you heard from me, keep as the pattern of sound teaching, with **faith and love** in Christ Jesus. Guard the good deposit that was entrusted to you—guard it with the help of the Holy Spirit who lives in us (2 Timothy 1:13-14).*

Paul tells Timothy to guard the good deposit entrusted to him—in other words, the good news that Jesus Christ came into

---

29 This is the Latin motto found on the seal of Milligan College, Tennessee. Alternate pronunciation of *Age* is *AH-jay.*

the world, he lived among the created, and out of his great love for his people, died on the cross so that there might be atonement for sin. We too, must guard the gospel message that has been entrusted to us and we, me! and you!—must act for God with faith and love.

So now, in obedience to the command of Christ to "Do This" let us, in faith and love, partake of the emblems of His body and His blood, broken and poured out for many for the forgiveness of sins.

Let us pray, acting for God with faith and love...

Faith, Hope, and Love
1 Corinthians 13:14

Faith is a gift of God. It is not a material that can be seen, heard, smelled, tasted or touched. But it is as real as anything that can be perceived with the senses. One can be aware of faith as easily as one can be aware of earth. Faith is as certain as the existence of water. Faith is as sure as the taste of an apple, the fragrance of a rose, the sound of thunder, the sight of the sun, the feel of a loving touch.

Hope is a wish, a longing for something not now possessed, but with the expectation of receiving it. Faith adds surety to hope.

—S. Jack Holloway[30]

In the first Corinthian epistle, Paul closes his famous love chapter: *And now these three remain: faith, hope and love. But the greatest of these is love (I Corinthians 13:13).* This table fellowship represents elements of all three: faith, hope and love.

Faith. Faith in God who creates, sustains, redeems.

---

30 S. Jack Holloway, letter written to his son, Clinton J. Holloway, February 20, 1998. Meditation written for my Ordination to the Christian Ministry, May 31, 1998.

Hope. Hope in the salvation purchased by his death. Hope in his eventual return.

Love. Love made manifest in the incarnation of God as man. Love fully expressed on Calvary.

But the greatest of these is love. In his first epistle, John writes: *This is how we know what love is: Jesus Christ laid down his life for us (I John 3:16).*

Let us pray, remembering that the greatest of these is love...

KOINONIA
REVELATION 19:7

The Greek word for communion is *koinonia (coy-no-NEE-ah)*. Koinonia is a very rich word in the ancient Greek language, full of meaning. The word is used for fellowship we enjoy around the Lord's table when we partake of the emblems. It is also the word used for the table fellowship we enjoy when we have our fellowship dinners, as the ancient church was accustomed to doing. Koinonia is also the word used in the Greek for the marriage relationship. You will remember Christ called himself the bridegroom and the church his bride. In all of these meanings koinonia conveys a give and take relationship. Each side contributes something beneficial to the other parties in the relationship.

Christians observe the Lord's Supper to respect and renew a relationship. Christ gave his life as an atoning sacrifice for the sins of the world. In return we give him our love, our adoration, and our worship. We give our tithes and offerings and these are used to build his kingdom on earth. We give him our lives and he promises to take us to live with him and the Father and the Holy Spirit for eternity. It is a give and take relationship, beneficial to both God and man.

In preparing our hearts to take this supper we worship him

and prepare ourselves for his coming. In the book of Revelation, John writes: *Let us rejoice and be glad and give him glory! For the wedding of the Lamb has come, and his bride has made herself ready (Revelation 19:7).*

As we pray, make yourself ready....

Do This!

1 Corinthians 11:23-26

In 1953, when Queen Elizabeth II was to be crowned the sovereign monarch of the British Empire, invitations were sent to a distinguished lot: Dukes, Barons, Lords, noblemen and women of every title and form, members of the government and of the Church, and even representatives of the common people. No matter the importance and rank of the person, each invitation bore this closing statement: "All excuses ceasing." This was an invitation to a celebration for which there was no legitimate reason for being absent. For you see, when royalty issues an invitation it is an extraordinary matter.

At this moment we celebrate at the invitation of another Sovereign Monarch—one much more important than Queen Elizabeth. On the night he was betrayed the King of Kings called together the Twelve. By all accounts, they were a motley crew of fishermen, radicals, even a tax collector. When they were at the table he commanded them, "Do this!" in remembrance of me. With these words, he extended an invitation not only to those twelve, but to all who would come after and believe in him. It is an invitation to all of us to be with him, not only on the first day of the week, but for eternity. Who else can make such a grand invitation? And who could say no? Because when royalty issues an invitation it is an extraordinary matter.

The Lord Jesus, on the night he was betrayed, took bread, and when he had given thanks, he broke it and said, "This is my body, which is for you; do this in remembrance of me." The same way, after supper, he took the cup, saying, "this is the new covenant in my blood; do this, whenever you drink it, in remembrance of me." For whenever you eat this bread, and drink this cup, you proclaim the Lord's death until he comes (I Corinthians 11:23-26).

Let us pray, accepting the King's invitation to come...

Grace Stooped Down
John 1:14-17

It has been said:

"Love that reaches up is adoration.

Love that reaches out is affection.

Love that reaches down is grace."[31]

We have within ourselves the capacity for all three. We lift up our hands and hearts in adoration to the Father. We reach out to one another in the body of Christ with affection. And when we reach down to help "one of the least of these," we show the world a bit of grace.

This love is but a dim reflection of the grace God has shown us. In the Gospel according to John are recorded these words that testify to the grace of our Lord: *The Word became flesh and made his dwelling among us. We have seen his glory, the glory of the One and Only, who came from the Father, full of grace and truth.*

John testifies concerning him. He cries out, saying, "This was he of whom I said, 'He who comes after me has surpassed me because he was before me.'" From the fullness of his grace we have all received one blessing after another. For the law was given

---

31 Attributed to Pastor and Biblical Scholar Donald Barnhouse.

through Moses; grace and truth came through Jesus Christ (John 1:14-17).

The Law was given by God through Moses. Like any law there was punishment for transgression. In the Law of Moses there is little room for grace. The price of sin was exacted in the sacrifice of life. A pigeon, a lamb, a heifer, or your own life, if your sin was great enough! But God knew from the start that his people could not make it alone, on their own account. So he sent Grace. Grace stooped down and wrapped himself in flesh and, for a time, dwelt among us. And at the appointed hour Grace was nailed to a tree. The price of the sin of the world was exacted in the sacrifice of his life. Thus, the love that reaches down is the fulfillment of the Law! (Matthew 5:17).

We have all received one blessing after another from the fullness of his grace. Let us give thanks and pray...

Profundity in Simplicity
Luke 22:15-19

Sometimes the most profound concepts come to us in simple forms. School children are taught Einstein's Theory of Relativity with the simple equation $E=MC^2$. But who among us can explain the theory behind the equation, that motion, time, and space are not absolute and that time is a dimension?

Love is another profound concept. Who can explain all of its intricacies and subtle nuances? But somehow it is easily understood in the form of a hug, the gift of a flower, or a grandmother insisting you have something to eat before you "rush off."

The Passover was a big concept for the Jewish nation. It was symbolic of freedom, the provision of the Lord in times of trial, and of His guidance in the wilderness. Yet the Passover was a simple meal, recalling the one prepared in haste the night the Lord struck down the firstborn of Egypt.

The Jews had gathered in Jerusalem for the Passover. Jesus and the disciples gathered in the upper room. During the meal Jesus took simple items, the cup and the bread, and invested them with a significance far surpassing our concepts of time, motion, and space. He gave them a meaning greater than the remembrance of the Passover. And He showed us a greater love than the world had ever known.

And he said to them, "I have eagerly desired to eat this Passover with you before I suffer. For I tell you, I will not eat it again until it finds fulfillment in the kingdom of God."

After taking the cup, he gave thanks and said, "Take this and divide it among you. For I tell you I will not drink again of the fruit of the vine until the kingdom of God comes."

And he took the bread, gave thanks and broke it, and gave it to them, saying, "This is my body given for you; do this in remembrance of me" (Luke 22:15-19).

Let us pray, thanking God for such profundity that comes in such simplicity...

One With the Father
John 17:20-21

Missionary David Giles tells the following story about his father, Ray Giles.[32] One day, while waiting for the school bus to come, young Ray went out behind the house to where his father was plowing the potato patch. The boy stood there for several moments, saying not a word. When his father came to the end of the row he asked Ray, "What is it that you want?" The child answered, "I don't want anything, but to be with you!"

The child wanted nothing more than to be with his father. How much more should we as the children of God desire only to be in the presence of our heavenly Father? On the night he was betrayed, Jesus earnestly prayed we might be one with the Father and the Son. John records his prayer, first for the disciples, and then for all believers: *"My prayer is not for them alone. I pray also for those who will believe in me through their message, that all of them may be one, Father, just as you are in me and I am in you.* **May they also be in us** *so that the world may believe that you have sent me" (John 17:20-21).*

---

32 Ray Giles and his wife, Effie, served several decades as missionaries with Christian Missionary Fellowship.

Jesus wanted nothing more than for all of God's children to be in the presence of the Father. To make this possible the Father sent his Son to earth to save the lost children, first by sharing the good news and then by giving up his life as the atoning sacrifice for sin. As we pray and partake of this memorial meal, clear your heart and your mind, shut out all the clutter of the world that distracts us from our purpose, and meditate on this gift. If it is your prayer today, tell the Father, "I don't want anything, but to be with you."

Let us pray, seeking to be one with the Father...

The Greatest of These is Love
Matthew 22:37-40

A great and wise teacher of the Law was once asked to give a summary of all the teachings of the Law and the Prophets. The Rabbi answered with the words of Jesus, *"'Love the Lord your God with all your heart and with all your soul and with all your mind.' This is the first and the greatest commandment. And the second is like it: 'Love your neighbor as yourself.' All the Law and the Prophets hang on these two commandments"* (Matthew 22:37-40).

"When **you do this**," the Rabbi added, "everything else is commentary!"

But how do **we** know what love is? The Apostle whom Jesus loved tells us. *This is how we know what love is: Jesus Christ laid down his life for us. And we ought to lay down our lives for our brothers (1 John 3:16).*

When **you do this,** everything else is commentary!

Let us pray, giving our love to God with all of our heart, soul, and mind...

Veritas Vos Liberabit
John 8:32

Don't tell anyone, but the seal of Bluffton High School, a public high school in Indiana, carries within it one of the most fundamental tenets of Christianity.[33] On the seal, above an open book is the Latin phrase *Veritas Vos Liberabit (VEH-ree-tas vohs lih-ber-AH-bit).* Few probably give much thought to its meaning.

Veritas Vos Liberabit. Thomas Jefferson inscribed it over the gateway to the University of Virginia. Frederick Doyle Kershner, a leading Disciple educator of the first half of the twentieth century, said "these words embody the ultimate ideals of both education and democracy."

But just what does this phrase mean? You may have surmised from the open book pictured on the seal that it is from the Bible. *Veritas Vos Liberabit* means *The Truth Will Make You Free.* The verse is John 8:32 which says, *"And you shall know the truth and the truth shall make you free."*

Education and academic circles will say it is Learning and Education that will set you free from ignorance and a life of drudgery. But knowing and believing in the real **truth** sets you

---

33 The high school that the author attended.

free from the bondage of sin and provides freedom from a life of guilt and shame.

Again, John writes, *Jesus said unto him, "I am the way, the truth, and the life: no man cometh unto the Father but by me"* (*John 14:6; KJV*).

Veritas Vos Liberabit. Jesus Christ is the personification that "the truth will make you free." To know the truth is to abide in the truth and to commune with the truth. Just now, we are privileged to partake of the symbols of the body and blood of the truth. By that truth we are enabled to come unto the Father so we might dwell with him in glory, forever.

Let us pray, being made free by the truth...

CALL NOW! THERE ARE NO OBLIGATIONS...
ROMANS 8:12-14

There was an interesting commercial on Christian radio. It was the humorous story of a man who was driving down the highway, going merrily about his business. Suddenly, a car appeared out of nowhere and hit him head on. He was killed and instantly floated to heaven on a pillowy white cloud playing a harp. He stood before Saint Peter and the Pearly Gates and demanded admission into Heaven on the grounds that he had been a good person.

"Sorry," was Saint Peter's reply, checking his records, "Nobody here by that name."

"What do you mean nobody by that name?" he questioned. "It must be a computer error. I was a good person. I gave to charity. Check again, my name has to be there." He was quickly growing impatient.

Finally, after a long and careful search, Saint Peter says again, "I'm sorry, but there is nobody listed here by that name."

"You have got to be to be kidding me!" the man exclaimed. "After all the good things I did? I even went to church!!!"

At that, Saint Peter pushed a button, the floor opened up, and you heard a *swoosh* as the man dropped to Hell.

The commercial ended with "Don't let this happen to you.

Dial 1-824-NEED-HIM. **Call Now! There are no obligations!"**

Funny as it may be, one of the problems with this situation is some people believe all you need to do to get into Heaven is be a good person, give to charity, and go to church. But the real tragedy is in the "**Call Now! There are no obligations!"** Many people only want a religion with no obligations. They seek a religion where there are no demands on their time, they are not called upon to make sacrifices, and they are not expected to give up a life of sin.

Paul writes to the church in Rome: *Therefore, brothers, we have an obligation—but it is not to the sinful nature, to live according to it. For if you live according to the sinful nature, you will die; but if by the Spirit you put to death the misdeeds of the body, you will live, because those who are led by the Spirit of God are the sons of God (Romans 8:12-14).*

Christianity carries the obligation of putting to death our sinful nature and following the Spirit of God. And when we fail and need grace, we are obligated to come to Christ and the Cross of Calvary where he invites us to partake of his body and his blood for the forgiveness of sins.

Let us pray, asking to be led by the Spirit...

Come As You Are
Matthew 11:28-30

Perhaps you've received a postcard in the mail advertising a new church with a "come as you are" atmosphere. By this, they mean a relaxed atmosphere with no ties or fancy dresses. In other words, "Come in your sweats and hair curlers if you want!" While a comfortable worship atmosphere is appealing, I think they missed the point.

Whether we're wearing a designer suit or an out-of-date outfit, each of us comes to worship "just as we are." A church with a real "come as you are" atmosphere has less to do with the outside and more to do with the inside. It is not the condition of your clothing, but the condition of your heart, that matters. God does not care what we wear; He cares how sin weighs us down and keeps us from fellowship with him. He is concerned about souls that are wearied and heavy laden with guilt.

In the Gospel according to Matthew our Lord Jesus invites us to come to him just as we are. *"Come to me, all you who are weary and burdened, and I will give you rest. Take my yolk upon you and learn from me, for I am gentle and humble in heart, and you will find rest for your souls. For my yolk is easy and my burden is light" (Matthew 11:28-30).*

As we prepare now to partake of the Lord's Supper, come to him, just as you are. Lay your load of sin at his feet and find rest for your weary soul.

Let us pray, coming to him just as we are...

The Original Restoration Movement
Luke 22:17-19

Many in the Christian Churches and Churches of Christ take pride in our heritage as part of the Restoration Movement. For others, you say Restoration Movement and they think of rehabbing an old house. But I have news for you. Restoration was not an original idea with Barton Warren Stone, the Campbells, or other nineteenth-century Restoration Movement leaders. Nor was the idea a new one for John Calvin or Martin Luther when they sought to restore the church in the sixteenth century.

The very first record we have of a Restoration Movement takes place in the Garden of Eden. Adam and Eve had just eaten of the forbidden fruit. Then in shame they hid themselves among the trees and covered themselves with fig leaves. In the cool of the day, God went walking in the Garden. He called to man, "Where are you?" And since that very moment, God has sought to restore the relationship between Creator and Creation.

It was for the purpose of restoring man to God that Jesus left the splendor of heaven and dwelt among men. Jesus knew his earthly purpose was to atone for the sin of Adam and thus break down the barrier separating God and man. What was broken on earth, first in the Garden and since that time by every one of us, is to have restoration in heaven, through Jesus' death on the cross.

After taking the cup, he gave thanks and said, "Take this and divide it among you. For I tell you I will not drink again of the fruit of the vine until the kingdom of God comes."

And he took bread, gave thanks and broke it, and gave it to them, saying, "This is my body given for you; do this in remembrance of me" (Luke 22:17-19).

This is the original Restoration Movement!

Let us pray, seeking to restore fellowship with our Creator...

GREAT EXPECTIATIONS
JOHN 14:2-3

When the famed circus entertainer P.T. Barnum was a child, his father would often tell young Phineas that one day he would inherit a "most beautiful and valuable piece of property." Naturally, the child was eager and excited about his future prospects. One day the elder Barnum took his son to see the property. P.T. was disappointed to learn the beautiful and valuable real estate was actually a worthless swamp and he had been the victim of a cruel family joke. Perhaps that hoax was the source of Barnum's mastery of hype and circus showmanship?

This reminds me of another story about an important inheritance. Several times in the book of John, Christ tells his disciples his time with them is limited and he must soon return to his Father's house. But Christ also assures them that one day he will return to take them to his Father's house and to live with him forever. Jesus said, *"In my Father's house there are many rooms; if it were not so, I would have told you. I am going there to prepare a place for you. And if I go and prepare a place for you, I will come back and take you to be with me that you may also be where I am" (John 14:2-3).*

If you wear the name "Christian," you also share in this inheritance because you have been adopted into the family of God.

We are joint heirs with Jesus. Like young Barnum, we have every right to be eager and excited about our expected inheritance. However, we have the assurance that ours is not a swamp or a cruel joke, but our inheritance is **real** and will be more beautiful than we can imagine.

On the night Jesus made that promise he sealed it with his own blood, the blood of the new covenant. We remember that promise today, represented here by the bread and the cup, and eagerly anticipate the fullness of our inheritance in heaven. *For whenever you eat this bread and drink this cup, you proclaim the Lord's death until he comes (1 Corinthians 11:26).*

Let us pray with great expectations of our future inheritance...

OUT OF THE MOUTHS OF BABES
GALATIANS 5:24; ROMANS 6:6

Once upon a time, a boy about twelve years old went forward at invitation time. He told the minister he had come because he wanted "to be crucified."[34] The congregation chuckled at his innocent mistake, knowing he had come forward to be *baptized*. But was it a mistake? Was it a nervous mix-up in the vocabulary? Or was it an insight into the true purpose of baptism?

Paul reminds us in Galatians 5:24, *Those who belong to Christ Jesus have crucified the sinful nature with its passions and desires*. And in Romans 6:6, he writes, *For we know that our old self was crucified with him so that the body of sin might be done away with, that we should no longer be slaves to sin—because anyone who has died has been freed from sin*.

How do we crucify that sinful nature? We do it, in part, when we are obedient to Christ's commands and are baptized. The old sinful person is buried and the new life rises up out of the water to live for Christ. So it is appropriate, when coming to baptism, to say "I want to be crucified." It is appropriate to say, "I want to

---

34 This young boy was baptized at Gap Creek Christian Church, Elizabethton, Tennessee.

leave the death of sin and nail it to the tree, and I want to live with Christ."

As we come to this time of communion, we celebrate that life in Christ. We pause to reflect on his crucifixion for sin. This is a meal of communion and a meal of remembrance. And it is a meal of baptism, dying to sin each week and rising again in newness of life.

Let us pray, crucifying our sinful self with Christ who was crucified on Calvary...

Jehovah Jireh: The Lord Will Provide
Genesis 22:2, 13b-14

I am sure there were evenings when Abraham came out of his tent to stretch his old legs and get a breath of fresh night air. Standing there in the moonlight, the Canaanite sand beneath his feet, he would straighten up his aged frame and cast a wistful glance toward the heavens. Millions of stars twinkled in the darkness and he would gulp for a moment to catch his breath, remembering the covenant God had made with him.

It must have seemed just a dream that Abraham would be the father of many nations and his descendants would be as numerous as the stars in that sky. But God provided a son in Abraham's old age; God provided Isaac. And then God provided a test. He said, *"...Take your son, your only son, Isaac, whom you love, and go to the region of Moriah. Sacrifice him there as a burnt offering on one of the mountains I will tell you about" (Genesis 22:2).*

Instead of hesitating or questioning, Abraham did as the Lord had commanded. Isaac carried the wood for the burnt offering on his own back. On Mount Moriah Abraham bound the boy and laid him upon the altar of sacrifice.

But has God got a flair for timing! Just as Abraham was poised to kill his only son, God intervened and provided a ram instead.

*He went over and took the ram and sacrificed it as a burnt offering instead of his son. So Abraham called that place **The Lord Will Provide.**[35] And to this day it is said, "On the mountain of the Lord it will be provided" (Genesis 22:13b-14).*

Many years later, the city of Jerusalem grew up in this region. The story of Isaac foreshadows another important sacrifice that would take place here, only a short distance away, on Mount Calvary. This time, another one of Abraham's descendants, this one named Jesus, would be called to lie down on the altar of sacrifice. He too was an only son, beloved by His Father. But this time, God did not provide a ram to take his place. Instead, the Lamb himself was led to the slaughter. God did this in order to seal another covenant, that Jesus might provide salvation for all of Abraham's children and provide eternal life to all who come to the Father through the Son.

As we partake now of the elements which represent the blood and the body of the lamb that was slain, let them stand as a testament that God is Jehovah Jireh and on the mountain of the Lord it will be provided.

Let us pray, knowing the Lord will provide...

---

35 The Hebrew translation of *Jehovah Jireh* is *the Lord will provide.*

In the Cleft of the Rock
Exodus 33:17, 21-23

Have you ever been a little anxious? A little apprehensive? Needed a little extra assurance God was there? If you've ever longed to see God, you are in good company. Moses did too. It wasn't that he didn't believe—after all, he had met God in the burning bush and he watched God lead the Israelites out of Egypt with a pillar of fire. But every once in a while, he needed the reassurance that comes only with seeing God.

On one such occasion he asked of God, "Now show me your glory."

And the Lord said to Moses, "I will do the very thing you have asked, because I am pleased with you and I know you by name" *(Exodus 33:17) ...Then the Lord said, "There is a place near me where you may stand on a rock. When my glory passes by, I will put you in a cleft in the rock, and cover you with my hand until I have passed by. The I will remove my hand and you will see my back; but my face must not be seen" (Exodus 33: 21-23).*

We all have a bit of Moses in us. We know God. We believe in him. But every once in a while, we need to see him to be reminded he is there. If we are a little anxious, a little apprehensive, if we need a little assurance, all we need to do is ask. Jesus said,

"Ask and it will be given to you... For everyone who asks receives..." *(Matthew 7:7a and 8a).*

We will not see him face to face—not yet, anyway. But if we are willing we may see God anywhere. We will see him in the scriptures. We will see him in the fellowship of his children. We will see him in the cross. And finally we will see him in the loaf and the cup given by his son, Jesus Christ.

Beloved, in all circumstances, take heart. When you need re-assurance God is there, ask for him and you will see him. Just now, see God and his glory at this table. Each time you partake be reminded again of God's presence with us here until we see him face to face.

Remember the words that Fanny Crosby wrote so many years ago:

A wonderful Savior is Jesus my Lord,
He taketh my burden away;
He holdeth me up, and I shall not be moved,
He giveth me strength for each day.

When clothed in His brightness transported I rise
To meet him in clouds of the sky,
His perfect salvation, His wonderful love,
I'll shout with the millions on high.

He hideth my soul in the cleft of the rock
That shadows a dry thirsty land;

He hideth my life in the depths of his love,
and covers me there with his hand,
and covers me there with his hand.[36]

Let us pray, finding solace in the cleft of the rock...

---

36 *He Hideth My Soul,* Fanny J. Crosby, Public Domain.

His Blood be on Us
Matthew 27:19-25

When he was set down on the judgment seat, his wife sent unto him, saying, Have thou nothing to do with that just man: for I have suffered many things this day in a dream because of him. But the chief priests and the elders persuaded the multitude that they should ask Barabbas, and destroy Jesus. The governor answered and said unto them, Whether of the twain will ye that I release unto you? They said, Barabbas. Pilate saith unto them, What shall I do then with Jesus, which is called Christ? They all say unto him, let him be crucified. And the governor said, Why, what evil hath he done? But they cried out the more, saying, Let him be crucified. When Pilate saw that he could prevail nothing, but that rather a tumult was made, he took water, and washed his hands before the multitude, saying, I am innocent of the blood of this just person: see ye to it. Then answered all the people, and said, His blood be on us, and on our children (Matthew 27:19-25; KJV).

Little did the Jews realize, as they stood before the governor and answered "let his blood be on us and our children," that Christ came for this very reason. For this reason the Word became flesh and dwelt among us. For this reason he was baptized, tempted of

Satan, taught in the Synagogue, preached beside the sea, washed the disciples' feet, healed the leper, and ate with the tax collector. For this reason he gathered with the disciples in the upper room, broke the bread, poured out the cup and prayed. For this reason he stood before Pontius Pilate, was mocked by Herod Antipas, was beaten by the Roman guard and surrendered his body to the cruel cross. For this reason he wore the crown of thorns, was crucified, had his side pierced and died. For this reason he was buried, descended into Hell, and on the third day rose again.

This is the reason: so his blood could be on us, and on our children; so by his blood we would be saved and so we can look forward to living with the Father, and the Son and the Holy Spirit, forever! Amen!

Let us pray, asking that his blood be on us and our children...

THE LAST WILL AND TESTAMENT OF JESUS CHRIST
MATTHEW 26:26-29

Often a loved one will give us some keepsake or leave us some treasure when they pass away; after they are gone this object becomes our reminder of them. Perhaps it is a china cup, a watch, a plate, or a painting. Whatever it is, these treasures come to represent that loved one. We value that item far more than its monetary worth because seeing it or holding it reminds us of the person who touched our life. That one memento comes to represent everything the loved one meant to us.

Have you ever read the **Last Will and Testament of Jesus Christ**? It is in the Bible, you know. While it does not start out, "I, Jesus Christ, being of sound mind and body...," it should be just as familiar to you. Although Jesus, together with his Father, owns all of the vastness and the riches of the universe, Jesus left only two items in his will. Jesus gave the only two things he owned while he lived on earth: his body and his blood.

While they were eating, Jesus took bread, gave thanks and broke it, and gave it to his disciples, saying, "Take and eat; this is my body."

Then he took the cup, gave thanks and offered it to them, saying, "Drink from it, all of you. This is my blood of the covenant, which is poured out for many for the forgiveness of sins. I tell you, I will not drink of this fruit of the vine from now on until that day when I drink it anew with you in my Father's kingdom" (Matthew 26:26-29).

In his "last will and testament," Jesus left us the bread and the cup. We received them, just before his death, as a reminder of his many gifts to us: love, mercy, grace, joy, peace, and more. These emblems represent Jesus' promise of eternal life. And we value them more than great riches because they represent everything Jesus means to us.

Let us pray, remembering the gift Christ gave us when he died...

NE OBLIVISCARIS
LUKE 22:17-19

The celebrated and sometimes hated Clan Campbell of the Scottish Highlands are known for their bravery as much as their barbarous deeds.[37] The Campbell family motto is *Ne Obliviscaris (nay ah-bliv-iss-CAR-iss)*; it is a Gaelic phrase which means *Lest We Forget.* The motto calls Campbells scattered around the world to remember their proud Highland heritage.

Lest We Forget is also a theme echoed in that old hymn of the faith *Lead Me to Calvary.*

> *King of my life I crown Thee now—Thine shall the glory be;*
> *Lest I forget Thy thorn-crowned brow, lead me to Calvary.*
> *Lest I forget Gethsemane, Lest I forget Thine agony,*
> *Lest I forget Thy love for me, Lead me to Calvary.*[38]

The memorial meal laid before us is a weekly reminder to focus our attention back on Calvary. We do this lest we forget the proud

---

37 The author's Mother is a proud descendant of that ancient Highland family, The Campbells of Argyll.
38 *Lead Me to Calvary,* Jennie Evelyn Hussey, copyright 1921, renewal 1949 by Hope Publishing Company.

heritage we have as Christians. We do this lest we forget the sacrifice that was made. We do this lest we forget Christ commanded we remember him in this way.

After taking the cup, he gave thanks and said, "Take this and divide it among you. For I tell you I will not drink again of the fruit of the vine until the kingdom of God comes."

And he took bread, gave thanks and broke it, and gave it to them, saying, "This is my body given for you; do this in remembrance of me" (Luke 22:17-19).

Let us pray, lest we forget...

Quid pro Quo
1 John 3:16, John 6:51

We are now facing a divine encounter, sacred commerce, a transaction across time and temporality. God acts in the Lord's Supper. This is life for life. Quid pro Quo. Jesus gave his life for us and we are filled. In return we give our life for Him. We give our life *to* Him.[39]

Paul said, *This is how we know what love is: Jesus Christ laid down his life for us. And we ought to lay down our life for our brothers (1 John 3:16).*

Jesus said, *"I am the living bread that came down from heaven. If anyone eats this bread, he will live forever. This bread is my flesh, which I will give for the life of the world" (John 6:51).*

Let us pray, giving ourselves to him, as he gave himself for us...

---

39 Special thanks to Dean E. and Dorothy K. Walker for this understanding of the Lord's Supper. Dean Walker was a former President of Milligan College and founder of Emmanuel School of Religion (Tennessee).

Debts of Love
Romans 13:8

An old story concerns a father, his young son and the paying of debts. Often the father would come into the room where his son was playing and would say to him, "Come Bobby, it is time to pay your debts." The little boy would happily climb into his father's lap, throw his arms around his father's neck, bury his soft cheek in his father's rough beard, and begin to hug and kiss his father with all his might. An observer to this little family ritual puzzled, "Is that how little Bobby pays his debts?" "Yes," was the father's answer, "All he can do to pay his debts is to love his father and he loves me just as hard as he can." Bobby's parents clothe and feed him. They watch him day and night and work hard to give him a happy home. How can the little boy repay his father for all of this kindness and care? He pays his debts with love.

In scripture debt describes not only situations involving money; debt also illustrates the place of sin in our lives. When Jesus taught his disciples to pray he taught them to ask the Father for forgiveness of the debt of sin. He also taught them our sins are forgiven as we forgive others. *"Forgive us our debts, as we have forgiven our debtors" (Matthew 6:12).* The Galatian Epistle says the same thing when Paul sums up the Law and the Prophets with five words: *Love your neighbor as yourself (Galatians 5:14).*

Throughout scripture there is a corollary between debts and sin, between forgiveness and love. Jesus told the story of two men who owed debts to a money lender (Luke 7:41-43). One owed 500, the other owed fifty. Neither man could afford to pay his debts so the money lender forgave both debts. Which of them, Jesus asked, will love more? The answer? The one forgiven most will be the one to love more.

We can see ourselves in Bobby, the little boy. We can see ourselves in the two men whose debts were forgiven. We have debts we cannot pay. We have sinned and fallen short of what is required. But when we come to this table and seek forgiveness the balance due is wiped away; our debt is forgiven.

How? The answer is love. *This is how we know what love is: Jesus Christ laid down his life for us. And we ought to lay down our lives for our brothers (I John 3:16).* The payment of debt is freely given in love to all who seek it. The only requirement is we give back as we have received, that we forgive as we have been forgiven, that we love as we have been loved.

Romans 13:8 says, *Let no debt remain outstanding, except the continuing debt to love one another, for he who loves his fellow-man has fulfilled the law.*

Let us pray, asking the Father to give all of us more and more love with which to pay our debts…

Love Covers a Multitude of Sins
1 Peter 4:7-8

The end of things is near. Therefore be clear minded and self-controlled so that you can pray. Above all, love each other deeply, because love covers a multitude of sins (1 Peter 4:7-8).

The end of all things is near. How near we do not know but we do know that one day soon Christ will return for his bride, the Church. Peter tells us in this epistle to be ready, to be clear minded, to pray, and most of all to love. For above all else love will show the church's ownership by the master.

Love covers over a multitude of sins, according to Peter. In fact love covers over all sins when we remember it was the love of the bridegroom for his bride that sent the son to earth to surrender his life on Calvary.

Let us pray, giving thanks that Love covers the multitude of sins…

The Hiding Place
Psalm 91:1-2

The Dutch city of Haarlem is located near the North Sea. If you visit this city, you can see the home of Corrie ten Boom, made famous by her book *The Hiding Place.* During the Second World War the Ten Boom family participated in the Dutch Resistance to Hitler's Nazi regime. They even went so far as to build a hiding place in their home to shelter Jews.

The hiding place was less than three feet wide and only about eight feet long. It was built for a maximum capacity of eight people standing front to back. During a Nazi raid the Jews staying in the house had less than one minute get into the hiding place through a secret door in the back of a shelf measuring less than 24 by 30 inches wide. Can you imagine getting six to eight people through such an opening and into a small space in under 60 seconds?

In spite of this, the day the Ten Boom house was raided six Jews found safety in this secret place. Six lives were saved. But the Ten Boom family was not so fortunate; four of the Ten Boom family died for this service to the Lord. Another family member, Corrie ten Boom, was eventually released from the concentration camp through a clerical error. Following her release Corrie spent the next 30 years as what she called a "Tramp for the Lord," preaching the love of God around the world.

Corrie later wrote about an incident in the concentration camp which she tells helped her find a hiding place in God. "It is evening, about 30 of God's children are standing or sitting between the barracks..." she wrote. "Bep (her sister—Betsie) is reading Psalm 91, *He who dwells in the secret place of the Most High shall abide under the shadow of the Almighty. I will say of the Lord, "He is my refuge and my fortress; My God, in Him will I trust..."* The barracks are so ugly and the barbed wire so horribly visible everywhere, but wagtails and skylarks are sitting in the birch trees and over all this is spread God's beautiful firmament with its magnificent colors which proclaim his handiwork."[40]

Amidst the horrors of the Holocaust, God never abandoned Corrie ten Boom; though she was in a death camp she was able to find comfort and communion with her Savior. In him she found her hiding place.

The message is the same for us. Despite the struggles we face in life, God is also our refuge, our fortress, in whom we can put our trust. In this communion he invites us to abide under the shadow of the Almighty and find within him our own hiding place.

Let us pray: thank you for being our refuge, our fortress, our hiding place...

———⁂———

40 Ten Boom, Corrie, *Prison Letters* Flemming H. Revell Co., Old Tappan, N.J., 1975, page 74.

I Am the Light of the World
John 8:12

There can be little doubt the world changed on September 11, 2001. Smoke rose from the burning Pentagon and clouds of dust and debris filled the air as the World Trade Center's towers came crashing down. In horror, we watched the drama unfold and we could do nothing. Darkness gripped our hearts and choked out the light just as the smoke of tragedy hid the sun.

The night after this tragedy, the members of First Christian Church, Nashville, Tennessee gathered in their sanctuary for prayer just as the sun set in the west. They watched as the shadow of darkness crept across the stained glass Window of Crucifixion and the central figure of the crucified Christ grew dark. At the same time, on the other side of the sanctuary, they watched as the Window of the Risen Savior was brilliantly filled by the light of evening sun. They realized even in the darkness of Christ's crucifixion, the greatest tragedy of human history, glorious light still illuminated the hope of his resurrection.[41]

Jesus said, *"...I am the light of the world. Whoever follows me*

---

41 The Window of the Crucifixion and the Window of the Resurrection are in the former sanctuary of First Christian Church, Nashville, Tennessee; now an auditorium of Franklin Road Academy.

will never walk in darkness but will have the light" (John 8:12). The Lord's Supper reminds us Jesus Christ is the light of the world. Be drawn to the promise resurrection through this memorial meal, and as you bear his name be a reflection of his light and his love to a dark and hurting world.

Let us pray, asking the Light of the World to cast out all our darkness…

WHAT DOES A HANDKERCHIEF SAY ABOUT LOVE?
ROMANS 5:8

Did you ever wonder what a handkerchief says about love? Dr. Henry Derthick, one-time president of Milligan College, used his handkerchief to convey a message of love. He would wave his handkerchief up and down three times for I...Love...You! *[Wave handkerchief up and down three times.]* Anyone who saw Dr. Derthick's handkerchief fluttering up and down immediately understood the message of love he was demonstrating.

Dr. Yoon Kwon Chae of the Korea Christian Gospel Mission in Seoul and director of the Geon Children's Home wrote this about his own handkerchief:

"Perhaps the dirtiest thing on earth is my handkerchief. It is always wet with children's tears, snot, snivel, candy spills, etc. People probably do not want to borrow it, but I do not mind carrying it in my pocket. Actually, I am proud to carry it in my pocket, except when I use it for illustrations ...then I spread germs all over the front pews. I really feel like Christians should be like dirty handkerchiefs, wiping the filth of this world. It is not valued, it is not respected, but without it this world will remain dirty."[42]

---

42 Adapted from Yoon Kwon Chae, Korea Christian Gospel Mission, Seoul, Korea, taken from his mission newsletter, citation unknown.

Dr. Chae closes, "So, Christians, TRY TO BE HANDKER-CHIEFS OF THIS WORLD!" It's such a simple thing—a 15x15 inch piece of fabric—but what a message of love it can demonstrate, whether it says "I...Love...You" *[wave handkerchief]* or it dries the tears of the hurting and sick.

In the same way, love is demonstrated in the table spread before us. The bread is the symbol of the broken body of Jesus and the cup is the symbol of his blood. Together they are symbols of God's eternal message to us: I...Love...YOU (*wave handkerchief*). Romans 5:8 (NKJV) tells us: *But God demonstrates his own love for us in this: While we were still sinners, Christ died for us.*

Let us pray: Let us be the handkerchiefs of this world...

It is Well With My Soul
Psalm 55:18

It Is Well With My Soul is a familiar and beloved hymn to many North American Christians. It was written in 1873 at a time of great personal tragedy for the writer, Horatio Spafford.[43] When Spafford wrote the words, he and his family had just survived the Great Chicago Fire only to lose his four daughters during a ship wreck in the north Atlantic. It begins:

> *When peace like a river attendeth my way,*
> *When sorrows like sea billows roll—*
> *Whatever my lot, Thou hast taught me to say,*
> *It is well, it is well with my soul.*

Horatio Spafford wrote those words one lonely night while sailing in another ship passing over the spot where his daughters drowned. He was not writing as a happy-go-lucky spirit or an overly optimistic Pollyanna; instead he wrote as one who had by trial-tested faith come to believe in the assurance that has come to us from Jesus.

43 *It Is Well With My Soul,* Horatio G. Spafford, Public Domain.

My sin—O the bliss of this glorious thought—
My sin, not in part, but the whole,
Is nailed to the cross, and I bear it no more:
Praise the Lord, praise the Lord, O my soul!

Horatio Spafford could have been crushed by this tragedy, but instead he claimed this promise in Psalm 55:18: *He hath delivered my soul in peace from the battle that was against me (KJV)*.

Weekly we celebrate that same assurance when we come to the Table. The death of Jesus on the cross, his body broken and his blood shed seals that promise! Beloved, celebrate that assurance; rejoice in the promise! Our sin, not in part, but the whole, has been nailed to the cross and we bear it no more!

Let us pray:
And, Lord, haste the day when my (our) faith shall be sight,
The clouds be rolled back as a scroll:
The trump shall resound and the Lord (YOU) shall descend,
"Even so"—it is well with my soul.

The Unity We Share at the Table
Selections of John 17:20-23

Two hundred years ago, Thomas Campbell, a spiritual forefather of the Restoration Movement, looked around and saw the sin of division separating Christians one from another and destroying the fellowship God intended for his children. He wrote in the *Declaration and Address:*

(Prop.1) THAT the church of Christ upon earth is essentially, intentionally, and constitutionally one; consisting of *all* those in *every* place that profess their faith in Christ and obedience to him in all things according to the scriptures...

(Prop.2) That although the church...must necessarily exist in particular and distinct...(congregations), locally separate one from another; yet there ought to be...no uncharitable divisions among them. They ought to receive each other as Christ hath also received them to the Glory of God...[44]

Two thousand years ago, Jesus looked around and saw the division

---

44 Thomas Campbell, *Declaration and Address,* Brown and Sample, Washington, PA, 1809, 16 (emphasis mine).

of sin was separating God's creation from Him and was destroying the fellowship God intended his children to have with the Father. Praying on the night before he was crucified, Jesus said,

*I pray...for those who will believe in me..., **that all of them may be one, Father, just as you are in me and I am in you. May they also be in us** so that the world may believe that you have sent me...**May they be brought to complete unity** to let the world know that you sent me and have loved me **even as you have loved them.*** [45]

The mission of Christ was to bring **us** into that Father-Son oneness so we could enjoy the completeness of God's love. Though we must worship in different congregations geographically separate from one another, there should be no unbiblical and uncharitable divisions between us. From Jesus' prayer we learn there should be no sinful division to keep us from true fellowship with one another and with God. Our love and unity should witness to the world.

Nowhere is the unity between Christians and God more evident than at this table. At this table we lay aside our divisions and we repent of our sins. At this table we share with each other as Christians and we share with our Father. This is Communion.

Let us pray: Make the unity we share at the table a reality in our times…

45 Selections from John 17:20-23, NIV (emphasis mine).

CLINTON J. HOLLOWAY • LEST WE FORGET

The Difference Between Hogs and Sheep
John 10:14-15

Do you know the difference between hogs and sheep? I know—at least, I thought I knew. Let me share with you a passage from a devotional reading by Charles Spurgeon, the famous nineteenth century preacher:

Sometimes, alas, sin even prevails over us, and we are forced in deep anguish to confess that we have fallen beneath its power. Who among us can say, "I am clean, I have not sinned?" Still a temporary defeat is not sufficient to effect a total subjugation. Sin shall not have dominion over the believer, for though he falls, he shall rise again.

The child of God when he falls into the mire is like the sheep that gets up and escapes the ditch as quickly as possible; it is not his nature to lie there. The ungodly man is like the hog that rolls in the filth and wallows in it with delight. The mire has dominion over the swine, but it has none over the sheep. With many bleating and outcries, the sheep seeks the shepherd again, but not the swine. Every child of God weeps, mourns, and bemoans his sin, and he hates it when for a while he has been overtaken by it. Sin has an awful power, but it has no dominion; it casts us down, but it cannot make us take delight in its evil.[46]

The unrepentant sinner is like a hog wallowing in the filth of the world. The child of God is like a sheep occasionally falling into a hole of sin but quickly trying to escape by calling to its shepherd for rescue.

Like those animals, we face a choice: we may delight in our sin or be disgusted by it. We may choose to wallow like the hog. But if we choose escape, we have a promise from Jesus, the great Shepherd, to rescue us quickly.

Jesus said, *"I am the good shepherd; I know my sheep and my sheep know me—just as the Father knows me and I know the Father—and I lay down my life for the sheep" (John 10:14-15).*

Let us pray: Good Shepherd, all we, like sheep have gone astray...

---

46 Charles Spurgeon, found in *Men of Character,* edited by Lawrence Kimbrough, Broadman & Holman Publishers, Nashville, TN., 2003, p. 69.

His Banner Over Me is Love
Song of Songs 2:4

Clint Holloway, the father of a toddler, writes:

"Much of my reading these days revolves around anthropomorphic animals: George, a curious monkey; Clifford, an oversized dog; and Hermie, a common caterpillar, to name a few. Children's books also fill the house. Andrew Peterson's *Slugs & Bugs & Lullabies* is the soundtrack to most of our meals. Psalty the Singing Songbook is our household background music. Elmo and The Wiggles or *Thomas the Tank Engine* dominate the DVD player. Unlike their parents, children have an amazing ability to listen to the same book, tape or movie over and over again without growing weary of it.[47] In fact, **Read**, **watch** and 'zic' (music) are probably my son's favorite words right now.

"Children's literature can provide wonderful devotional nuggets. A recent addition to our music repertoire included *His Banner Over Me is Love*. This simple but beautiful song reminds us

---

47 Psalty is a registered trademark of Ernie Rettino and Debbie Kerney Rettino. Elmo is a registered trademark of Sesame Workshop. The Thomas name and character is a registered trademark of Gullane (Thomas) Limited. The Wiggles is a registered trademark of The Wiggles PTY Ltd.

the King of Kings invites us to his banqueting table; there He displays His love for us as proudly as any army displays its colors or as any lover courts his beloved (Song of Songs 2:4).

"My toddler does not yet understand the meaning of these songs. To him, it may just be 'zic'. But the song is planting the truth of the cross in his mind, so I do not mind listening to it yet again. And amidst our busy lives it is a good reminder to his parents that *His Banner Over Me is Love!*"

Let us pray: Lord, you are my banner and the banner over me is love…

How Good and Pleasant it is
For Brothers to Dwell Together in Unity
Psalm 133:1

Psalms 120 through 134 are known as "Songs of Ascent." These Psalms, some traditions hold, were sung by the ancient Jews as they traveled to Jerusalem to worship at the Temple during feast times. Psalm 133 begins *Behold, how good and how pleasant it is for brothers to dwell together in unity!* (KJV). One commentator asks, "Isn't it a bit intriguing that such a Psalm would be sung by the people on the way to worship?" Did they sing to celebrate the reality of their worship together? Or perhaps they sang as encouragement to focus on God instead of things that divide us. Perhaps our own experience in worship might be different if, on our journey here, our families sang this song. *How good and pleasant it is for brothers to dwell together in unity.*

Perhaps Jesus also sang this song on his way to Jerusalem for his last Passover. *How good and pleasant it is for brothers to dwell together in unity.* Maybe he whistled the tune that night in the upper room when he broke bread with his friends for the last time. *How good and pleasant it is for brothers to dwell together in unity.* Surely it gave him comfort later that night when he prayed for the unity of his followers. *How good and pleasant it is for brothers to dwell together in unity.*

As we share together in the remembrance of Lord's Supper we demonstrate our oneness in him, proclaiming his death until he returns, sharing with the world a song of ascent, *How good and pleasant it is for the brothers and sisters in Christ to dwell together in unity...*[48] *For there the Lord commanded his blessing, even life forevermore (Psalm 133:3b).*

Let us pray: Lord, how good and pleasant it is when we dwell together in unity with you...

---

48 Adapted from a devotional by Wye Huxford, European Evangelistic Society.

The Extent of His Love
John 13:1, 17:20-23

In the Gospel of John, the thirteenth chapter, we find Jesus making preparations to close his earthly ministry. In verse one we read:

It was just before the Passover Feast. Jesus knew that the time had come for him to leave this world and go to the Father. Having loved his own who were in the world, he now showed them the full extent of his love (John 13:1).

Jesus instructed the disciples to prepare for the Passover Feast. At this celebration Jesus washed his disciples' feet, and he predicted Judas' betrayal and Peter's denial. Jesus comforted his disciples with the promise of the Holy Spirit. He also took bread and wine, common elements of any meal of the day, and made them symbols of his body and his blood.

Jesus told them, "This cup is the new covenant in my blood; do this, whenever you drink it, in remembrance of me."

In the seventeenth chapter of John we find Jesus in the garden following the Passover Feast and we learn about his love by his prayer for all believers.

I pray also for those who will believe in me through their message, that all of them may be one Father, just as you are in me and I am in you. May they also be in us so that the world may believe that you have sent me. I have given them the glory that you gave me, that they may be one as we are one: I in them and you in me. May they be brought to complete unity to let the world know that you have sent me and have loved them even as you have loved me (John 17:20-23).

When we participate in this new covenant by sharing the body and blood, we demonstrate our unity and remember the extent of God's love. We proclaim His love for those who are in Jesus, and we proclaim the hope that all who believe will share in that bond of love.

Let us pray, remembering the extent of his love...

Let Us Worship with Gladness
Psalm 122:1; Acts 2:46-47

I must admit, I love being at church! I love being here with all of you. And I love when we come together to truly worship. It is not difficult for me to understand what David meant when he wrote, *I was glad when they said to me "Let us go to the house of the Lord."* *(Psalm 121:1; NKJV).*

In the Book of Acts we find a description of the early church going to the house of the Lord: *Every day they continued to meet together in the temple courts. They broke bread together in their homes and ate together with glad and sincere hearts, praising God and enjoying the favor of all the people... (Acts 2:46-47).*

Did you catch that? **With glad hearts!** They, too, loved to gather for worship and fellowship.

At this time we break bread together. This is the central act of our worship because it is the time we come closest to God and enjoy communion with him as a family. Our hearts are glad, not because we remember the death of Jesus with our worship, but because death has been swallowed up in victory. Jesus once was dead but is alive again! For this reason, we gather with joy in the house of the Lord, and eat together of His meal with glad and sincere hearts.

Let us pray, worshipping with gladness...

LOST THINGS

LUKE 19:10

Luke's Gospel reminds us lost things matter to Jesus. Lost sheep, lost coins, lost sons; for that matter, all lost children. Jesus himself tells us, *"For the Son of Man came to seek and to save what was lost" (Luke 19:10).* Lost things were his mission.

We often think of this table as a family reunion. While that is true, some family members are not at this table, not at this reunion, because they are lost. Even as we gather, we ought to remember Jesus' mission: seeking and saving the lost.

Kei Eun Chang, minister of the Manchester Korean Christian Church in Manchester, New Hampshire, has written wonderfully about the challenge of the lost at this family reunion. He says, "As we remember and celebrate the Lord's Table each Sunday, we must also *remember* the mission of the church to those who are not around the Table; as we proclaim his death, we must remember Christ died for them as well." According to Kei Eun one of the purposes of this Sunday family gathering is to be "reenergized in our love for the Lord and the evangelistic passion of the church."[49]

---

49 Kei Eun Chang, *For the Sake of Gospel*, in *One Church: A Bicentennial Celebration of Thomas Campbell's Declaration and Address,* Edited by Glenn Thomas Carson, Douglas A. Foster and Clinton J. Holloway, Leafwood Press, Abilene, TX, 2008.

This reminds me of the sign at one Nashville church which says to those leaving the parking lot: YOU ARE NOW ENTERING THE MISSION FIELD.

On the night before his death, when Jesus prayed in the garden, he asked God for unity of the body *so that world may believe* (John 17:21). The world. All the world. Even in the last hours of life, lost things, lost people were on his mind. Church: as you partake of the body and blood of Christ be energized in the love of the Lord and his evangelistic passion for the lost.

Let us pray: Lord, help us look for lost things...

Canute's Crown
James1:12b

A thousand years ago a mighty king called Canute the Great ruled over much of northern Europe; he was a successful military leader and man of good common sense. Canute had many courtiers about him who were always vying for his attention by appealing to his vanity. Canute would walk into a room and the effusions would start.

"You are the greatest man who ever lived," would begin one.

"Your Highness, there is nothing you cannot do," another would add.

"Great Canute, monarch of all," another would sing. "Nothing in this world dares disobey you."

But since Canute was a man of much good sense he grew tired of hearing such foolishness. One day Canute was walking along the seashore and, as usual, the courtiers were at their hyperbolic praise. Canute had had enough; he would teach them a lesson and end the senseless flattery.

"So you say I am the greatest man in the world? And that all things obey me?" Canute asked.

"Absolutely," they said. "The world bows before you and gives you honor."

Canute ordered his chair brought to the edge of the sea and he sat down. He surveyed the ocean before him. "I notice the tide coming in. Do you think it will stop if I give the command?"

The courtiers were puzzled but they dared not say no. "Give the order, O great king, and the sea will obey," one of them assured.

"Very well, Sea!" cried Canute emphatically, "I command you to come no further. Waves stop your rolling! Surf! Stop your pounding! Do not dare to touch my feet!" He waited quietly a moment. Then the first tiny wave raced up the shore up and tickled his feet. "How dare you!" Canute shouted. "Ocean, turn back now! I have ordered you to retreat before me, and now you must obey! Go back."

Now, you know and I know (and Canute knew!) that was not going to happen. Another wave rushed up and curled around the king's feet. In a matter of moments the surf was up to his knees, soaking his royal robes. The tide came in just as it always does.

"Well, my friends," said Canute, "it seems I do not have quite as much power as you would have me believe. Perhaps you have learned something today. Perhaps now you will remember there is only one King who is all-powerful, and it is he who rules the sea and holds the ocean in the hollow of his hand. I suggest you reserve your praise for him."

Afterward, they say, Canute took off his crown and never wore it again, asserting there was no true king but Jesus.

There come times in our lives when we want make a fresh start, begin again, and we resolve to have new attitudes and actions. Perhaps we seek to refocus our Christian walk so that emphasis is on God and not on ourselves. This is a time to lay down our own crowns, like Canute, and pick up our crosses and follow Jesus, the true king. It is in doing that that we will all *receive the crown of life that God has promised to those that love him (James 1:12b)*.

Let us pray: Let us, like Canute, lay down our crowns in favor of the King of Kings...

I Am Loved
John 13:34b-35

Barnett Helzberg and Shirley Bush were engaged in 1967. Exhilarated at the thought of it, Barnett scribbled down three little words, "I AM LOVED." It is a wonderful feeling when you say to yourself, "I AM LOVED." And the feeling is more extraordinary when the sentiment comes from someone else. For Barnett Helzberg, the sentiment was so personal and heartfelt, that he almost didn't show his scribbling to anyone. But, to know that she said yes…to know that he was loved…Barnett was ecstatic! He wanted to tell the world; to share his joy!

The story would probably have ended here were it not for the fact that Barnett was the President of Helzberg Diamonds. Capitalizing on the wonderful feeling of knowing someone loves you, he created an advertising concept for his jewelry stores. Initially the company ordered 50,000 little red buttons with the words "I AM LOVED."[50] A newspaper advertisement launched the promotion using the soft-sell approach, "The age-old problem

---

[50] I AM LOVED and the red and white I AM LOVED BUTTON is a Registered Trademark of Helzberg Diamonds, The Helzberg Foundation. Above mediation adapted from the Helzberg Diamonds story found at www.iamloved.org/history. Stop by Helzberg Diamonds; the buttons are free for the taking… unfortunately, the diamonds are not!

hasn't changed. She still wants to know you love her. And you still wonder how to tell her." Almost immediately, the supply of buttons was exhausted and they rushed to order more. Demand for "I AM LOVED" buttons became a national movement after the Associated Press reported that the "latest craze to show your affection was to send your heroes, 'I AM LOVED' buttons." Thousands were sent overseas to soldiers in Vietnam. The advertising campaign put Helzberg Diamonds on the map. In the forty years since, over 50 million "I AM LOVED" buttons in a dozen languages have spread around the world.

The knowledge that we are dearly loved by God and loved by Jesus is the foundation of our Christian faith. "I live by faith in the Son of God," said the Apostle Paul in Galatians, "who loved me and gave himself for me" (Galatians 2:20b). Partaking of these elements representing the body and blood of Jesus, as we do each week, communing with Jesus and with each other, is like putting on Barnett Helzberg's little red button and affirming that extraordinary sentiment "I AM LOVED." And like Mr. Helzberg, the knowledge of that love exhilarates us, makes us ecstatic to share the good news with the world. Jesus said, *"As I have loved you, so you must love one another. By this all men will know that you are my disciples, if you love one another" (John 13:34b-35).*

Let us pray, thanking Jesus for this reminder that we are loved...

In Remembrance of Me
Isaiah 49:16; Deuteronomy 31:6

We probably all have at least one thing we are angry at God about: death, disease, war, famine, loneliness, abuse, injustice. Of all the issues of faith that someone can wrestle with, there is one thing that many people almost cannot forgive God for: Alzheimer's disease. For those who have seen its action in the life of a loved one, the pain is nearly unbearable. Let me read you a poem, a lament for an Alzheimer's victim.

In Remembrance of Me

They say it is a disease.

I say it is a thief who breaks in to steal;

who comes back again and again,

seeking who he may devour.

From the outside my house looks empty.

The windows have grown dark.

The fires of my hearth have gone cold.

I live in a house of sustained death.

But my soul still speaks with God.

My heart remembers.

I am engraved on the palms of his hands.[51]

He does not forget me.

God does not forget us; nor does he leave us or forsake us, whatever our condition or circumstance. God conveyed this promise through Moses, who at 120 years of age reassured Israel: *"Be strong and courageous. Do not be afraid or terrified because of them for the Lord your God goes with you; he will never leave you nor forsake you" (Deuteronomy 31:6).* God made that promise through Moses and he renewed it with Jesus. Each time we gather for the Lord's Supper we see again this physical reminder that he has engraved us on the palm of his hand and he does not forget us. Even in your doubt, pain, or anger he will never leave you or forsake you.

Let us pray: thank you for not forgetting us...

---

51 Isaiah 49:16. This poem was written in honor of Doris L. Campbell, an Alzheimer's victim.